Sculpture Parks
& Trails of England

Sculpture Parks & Trails of England

Alison Stace

A&C Black

This book is dedicated to my father.

First published in Great Britain in 2008
A & C Black Publishers Limited
38 Soho Square
London W1D 3HB
www.acblack.com

ISBN 13: 978-07136-7952-6
Copyright © Alison Stace 2008

CIP Catalogue records for this book are available from the British Library.

Book designer: Penny & Tony Mills
Cover designer: James Watson
Editor: Julian Beecroft
Research Assistant: Alison Evans
Regional Maps: Brian Southern

Cover images: (Top) *Angel of the North* by Antony Gormley at Gateshead. (Bottom, left to right) *The Brockhall Warrior* by Joanna Malin-Davies at Pride of The Valley Sculpture Park; *Ribbon of Colour* by Kate Maestri at Gateshead, *Double Oval* by Henry Moore at The Henry Moore Foundation, *Acrobats* by Barry Flanagan at the New Art Centre Sculpture Park, *Granite Catamarans on a Granite Wave* by Stephen Cox at Cass Sculpture Foundation, *Natural Circumference* by Dominique Bivar Segurado at Bergh Apton Sculpture Trail.

Printed and bound in China

left: *Swing Bridge* by Gerry Masse, 2003. Steel kinetic sculpture at Ironbridge Open-air Museum. *Photo by Alison Stace.*
far right: *Sitting Man* by Elizabeth Frink at Yorkshire Sculpture Park. *Photo by Jonty Wilde, courtesy of Yorkshire Sculpture Park.*

p.1: *Folded Leaves* by Graham Williams, stainless steel, at 'Art in the Garden' 2007, Sir Harold Hillier's Gardens.
p.2 & 3: *Broadside* by Rick Kirby, 2003. Mild steel. From the Hannah Peschar Sculpture Garden designed by Anthony Paul, landscape designer. *Photo courtesy of the Hannah Peschar Sculpture Garden.*

Acknowledgements

Thanks are due to all the sculpture parks, trails and gardens for their help in making this book possible. Thanks are due to the following people for their time, efforts and images, or permission for use of images; In the north I would like to thank Peter Sharpe at Kielder for his very thorough tour and information, Anna Pepperall and Kyoko Mae at Gateshead for their time, tour and information, Lucinda Compton of Newby Hall for taking time to explain their approach to the sculpture trail, Jan Wells at Yorkshire Sculpture Park for her time, images and information, Jon Bewley of Sustrans for his fantastic pictures and Alessia Macdonald for information, Tania Crockett for information and Katie Jarvis for images of Grizedale Forest Park, Lynn Smith at Norton Priory, Tony Trehy for information and images of Irwell Sculpture Trail, and Steve Messam of Fold for information on the Fred Festival.

In the Midlands I would like to thank Camilla D'Arcy-Irvine of Jerwood Sculpture Foundation for her help, thorough information and for supplying beautiful images, Carolyn Black for her time, tour and interesting discussion, Pam Brown of Ironbridge Open-Air Museum for her time and tour, Anne de Charmant of the Meadow Gallery for images and information, Jo Tinker at Burghley House for supplying great images, Alex Denbigh for the tour of Newnham Paddox Art Park, Michelle Bennett at Coventry Canal, Lucy Abel Smith at Quenington Sculpture Trust, and Chatsworth House.

In the South-east I would like to thank Michael Phipps and Emma Stower of the Henry Moore Foundation for their generosity with information and images, Antonia Crowhurst and Ed Wilde of Cass Sculpture Foundation for images and information, Hannah Peschar and Victoria at the Hannah Peschar Sculpture Garden, Eddie Powell for his tour and images of Pride of the Valley Sculpture Park, Amanda Thesiger at Stour Valley, Keith Collins for his time and pictures of Derek Jarman's Garden, Elizabeth Hodgson of 'Art in the Garden' and Joanna Selwood of Sir Harold Hillier's Garden, Rachel Bebb for her images of The Garden Gallery, Gordon Whittle of The Gibberd Garden, and Sally Leigh of Bergh Apton Sculpture Trail.

In the West Country I would like to thank Alice Houghton of the New Art Centre Sculpture Park and Gallery, Rinus van de Sande of Broomhill Art Hotel and Sculpture Gardens, Arwen Fitch at Tate St Ives and the generosity of the Hepworth Estate. Also Hannah Sofaer of the Portland Sculpture Quarry Trust, Sustrans (as before), and June Ashburner of the Mythic Garden.

I would also like to thank all the people that came with me to research various parks and gardens, and especially Alison Evans for all her help with general research and map reading. Thanks also to my mother for her editorial advice and thoughts, Julian Beecroft for his substanial pruning of the text and Penny Mills for her patience and lovely design of the whole book. Thanks also go to Brian Southern for his lovely regional maps, and to Joe Knight for his patience in revising maps of trails many times over. I would also like to thank the car for not breaking down on its many trips to Yorkshire and Devon over the last year and a half.

1

Newcastle upon Tyne

Carlisle

5 2a 2b

Middlesbrough

Kendall

6

Ripon

York

3

Preston

Leeds

Bury 8

4

Liverpool

Manchester

Runcorn 7

Chesterfield

18

Norwich

Telford

Leicester

14

Peterborough

12

29

Birmingham

16 15

Worcester

Kettering

Cambridge

10

Gloucester

Aylesbury

19 28 Harlow

11

17

Cirencester

23

LONDON

Bristol

34

Reading

Guildford

Bath

22 21

24

Barnstaple

31

Salisbury 30 27

Ashford

26

35

Southampton

20

25

Exeter

33

Bognor Regis

St Ives

Bill of Portland

32

Plymouth

Contents

Introduction

The reasons for writing this book were many. Firstly, the vast number of sculpture parks and trails around England seems to be one of the nation's best-kept secrets, even to many serious art lovers. Secondly, many keen walkers I know had not heard of some of these parks, and even after learning of their existence seemed to think they would be small, strange places full of odd sculptures appealing only to wealthy art buyers. The idea of the book, therefore, was to introduce a wider group of art lovers to the delights of outdoor sculpture in beautiful settings, many of which I felt were being overlooked simply due to lack of information. Equally, a large number of walkers could be introduced to accessible art in an unthreatening, non-gallery environment. Combining the two (art and landscape) is an ideal way to spend some of your weekend, providing a chance to see a variety of sculpture you would not necessarily see otherwise. The right sculpture and a suitable landscape tend to enhance each other.

The vast and very mixed assortment of sculpture parks and trails is a little bewildering, especially if you have never visited one before. Even an avid sculpture fan may be simply unaware that these places exist only a short journey away. For this reason, I thought that a small guide could be helpful in offering an overview of places to see sculpture in an outdoor setting. As well as featuring the most prominent and well-established, it also includes other places of interest which are much less well-known but which also have something to offer. Amongst these 'other places of interest', the size, the quality and the amount of sculpture varies enormously, and this guide aims to give you a good feel for each place so that you can decide what would suit you best, depending on your location, available free time and level of interest. I apologise in advance to any parks or trails that have been left out (or simply overlooked), but both budget and space were tight. I would be pleased to consider them for future inclusion if suitable.

For the more discerning sculpture buff, there is a distinction to be made between a sculpture park and a garden (and for that matter a trail), but there is not space here for the length of discussion this issue deserves. Broadly speaking, my interpretation is that the sort of sculpture found in a park tends to be on a monumental scale. It may address issues of land and nature, while actually being made from natural materials (such as work by Andy Goldsworthy), or in the right setting it may simply relate to and/or visually enhance the surrounding landscape. In a vast landscape such as Kielder, for example, it becomes a way to relate to and place yourself in the landscape, as well as a way to orientate yourself. At the Forest of Dean the question came up of whether it was a good idea to put a sculpture in a naturally beautiful spot, or whether it was better to place it in a less scenic environment, in order to encourage interest in and engagement with less appealing areas. This tactic has been used to great advantage in Gateshead, where *Threshold* (see p.24) has enlivened an otherwise derelict corner of the town.

Sculpture in gardens tends to be on a smaller, more domestic scale, and the work is perhaps more about how the individual relates to the space or makes it their own. Work in gardens tends to be more about personalising and enhancing a private area, whereas sculpture trails – again, the Forest of Dean is a good example – are often set up to encourage the visitor to explore and to navigate the landscape (usually, it's a wood) from point to point. Although at the Forest of Dean they are keen to point out that the journey is as important as the destination.

Each park, trail and garden is completely different, which does it make it hard to compare when some are publicly funded, while others are commercial ventures, but I have tried to give a clear summary of what you can expect

from each place. In view of this, I have tried to make honest but not overly harsh critiques.

Due to space, dimensions of work have not been included, they are not essential when the trees and space around the work gives a good indication of size. Maps have been included where necessary for places where maps were hard to obtain, or did not show artwork locations. Some were just too enormous to reproduce here, and most are easily obtained on site.

Above all, each trail and park is unique, with its own strengths and character. Ultimately, I hope this guide will go some way toward opening up the world of sculpture parks and trails to the large number of people who until now have quite simply been missing out.

above: View of pond and house at Hannah Peschar Sculpture Garden, with *Dewdrops* by Neil Wilkins in foreground. *Photo courtesy of Hannah Peschar Sculpture Garden (see p.102–6).*

The North-east

- Durham • Northumberland • Cleveland • Tyne &Wear
- Lancashire • Cheshire • W. Yorkshire • S. Yorkshire
- N. Yorkshire • East Riding

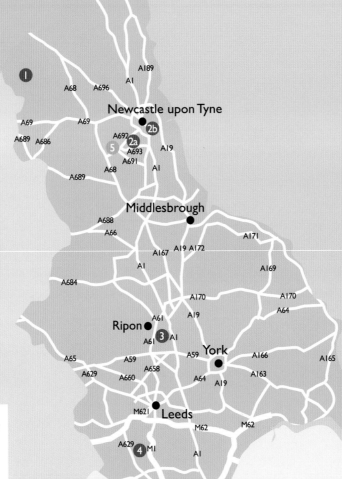

1 Art & Architecture at Kielder
2a Angel of the North
2b Art in Gateshead
3 Newby Hall Sculpture Park
4 Yorkshire Sculpture Park

Other Places of Interest

5 Consett to Sunderland

1 Art & Architecture At Kielder

Kielder Water & Forest Park, Northumberland

Information:

Kielder Partnership Tourist
Information Centre,
Main Street, Bellingham,
Northumberland, NE48 2BQ.
Tel: 01434 220643
www.kielder.org

Facilities: 3 cafés/visitor centres &
toilets. Also offers canoeing, sailing & mini
golf.
Open: All year
Admission: Free (car park £4, same ticket
can be used at all car parks).
Time needed: 2–3 days

Getting there

By road
From the south take the A1(M) north and
at Jctn 58 take A68 through Consett, turn
left onto A69 briefly and then right onto
A68 again. • Turn left (or right from the
north) off A68 towards Bellingham. •
Follow signs towards Falstone and
Kielder Water.

left: *Mirage*, (detail) by Kisa Kawakami, 2006.
Photo by Alison Stace.

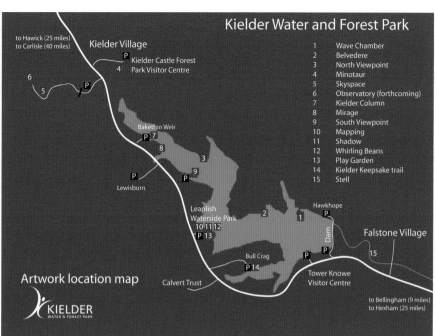

Kielder Water and Forest Park

1 Wave Chamber
2 Belvedere
3 North Viewpoint
4 Minotaur
5 Skyspace
6 Observatory (forthcoming)
7 Kielder Column
8 Mirage
9 South Viewpoint
10 Mapping
11 Shadow
12 Whirling Beans
13 Play Garden
14 Kielder Keepsake trail
15 Stell

to Hawick (25 miles)
to Carlisle (40 miles)

Kielder Village

Kielder Castle Forest Park Visitor Centre

Bakethin Weir

Lewisburn

Leaplish Waterside Park

Bull Crag

Calvert Trust

Hawkhope

Dam

Falstone Village

Tower Knowe Visitor Centre

to Bellingham (9 miles)
to Hexham (25 miles)

Artwork location map

KIELDER
WATER & FOREST PARK

Overview

Kielder Water and Forest Park is an enormous area of land and lake, with sculptures situated all around the lake itself – a total distance of 27 miles that doesn't include hiking off down little paths to see specific works that are tucked away. To do the place justice, and to fully appreciate the rural scenery and solitude, you really need three days here (probably two if you drive to the car park nearest each sculpture – there are several – and walk from there). The park is very well served by three different visitor centres. The main one, and the most central, is Leaplish Waterside Park, with accommodation on site and also mini-golf (which has been carefully designed as one of the sculptures!). Kielder-Castle visitor centre (originally an 18th-century hunting lodge) is next door to *Minotaur* (the maze sculpture) – or, to be more accurate, *Minotaur* has been constructed on the site of the lodge's old vegetable garden.

Kielder is actually a manmade lake, created originally as a reservoir to supply other areas

left: *Mirage*, by Kisa Kawakami, 2006. Consisting of shiny disks suspended in the trees. The wooden area below is a viewing platform. *Photo by Alison Stace.*
above: Map courtesy of Art & Architecture at Kielder.

with water in times of crisis. When it was built a large area including a railway line and many farms was flooded. Notice boards at viewpoints occasionally show you (somewhat creepily) where these were – or are – located beneath the surface of the lake.

The art programme at Kielder has been running for over ten years, and architectural pieces have been an integral part of it since 1999. A major new project, *Observatory*, will open early in 2008. Designed by Charles Barclay Archi-

tects, the piece is an enormous platform on stilts with open areas and rooms with telescopes from which to observe the stars. Apparently, the sky here is among the clearest and least light-polluted in England, making it an ideal location for astronomers.

Most of the work at Kielder is superb (especially the more recent pieces), and the location is stunning, making this one of the best of the sculpture parks. The sculpture helps to draw people out into the forest to engage with it in

some way, offering a new way of looking at or reflecting on it. The latest pieces of sculpture here are to be experienced rather than simply viewed as objects. As Peter Sharpe from the arts programme puts it, 'the actual physical sculpture is only two thirds of the project, the final third is the work being used and experienced by people, which fulfils and completes its purpose'. Be warned that in this part of the country it does rain a lot, and sometimes it can take a couple of hours to reach a sculpture – so be prepared and take provisions.

Finding your way around

It is now possible to print off detailed information sheets about each sculpture from the Kielder website, but be sure also to pick up the art & architecture pamphlet from one of the centres. You really need it to find all the pieces. Containing a map that gives a broad overview of the park (as shown here), it also offers more detailed maps to help locate each piece. More crucially for somewhere this large, it also gives an approximate walking time to each work from the nearest car park, as well as information about each sculpture.

There are a couple of ways to access sculptures. You can set off on foot along forest tracks from the nearest visitor centre. The sculptures are signposted with waymarkers, posts beside the path with an arrow pointing in the direction of a named piece. These are crucial to follow, as at times paths can criss-cross in all directions.

Alternatively, you can cheat a little by driving to the nearest car park and walking along forest tracks from there. If you have the time it is much nicer to walk. With so much ground to cover, even doing it on foot you may need to divide the area up into sections and drive to a different point each day, setting out from there. The actual

left: *Skyspace*, by James Turrell, 2000. The outside of the stone-built viewing chamber.
centre: *Skyspace*, view through the tunnel into the chamber.
right: *Skyspace*, looking up at the sky through the circular hole inside. *Photos by Alison Stace.*

Things to see

sculptures are not always signposted from the road, but the area will be named, and this is signposted, so check on the pamphlet maps for details and see the map on p.13 (for example, for the *Kielder Keepsake* you should park at Bull Crag).

In summer a ferry also runs across the lake to the *Belvedere*, and many other transport connections are being developed to make the north side of the lake more accessible. A new path is almost finished which will enable walkers, cyclists and horse riders to completely circumnavigate the lake. Currently, the north side can only be reached by tracks through the forest (or by the ferry in summer), as there is no road running along the north side. There has also been talk of putting in a tram to run the length of the north side.

The James Turrell *Skyspace* is a wonderful creation. A mile and a half from the Kielder Castle visitor centre (signposted from the car park), it takes approximately an hour to reach on foot, depending on your speed. James Turrell has been working with light for over 40 years, and the marvellous concept behind *Skyspace* has to be experienced to be appreciated. This one was built in 2000 and the only other that can be found in the UK, at the Yorkshire Sculpture Park (see p. 29), was built in 2007. These pieces are effectively shrines to light, evoking a sort of spiritual experience. In the case of the Kielder *Skyspace* it is a bit like visiting a temple, especially with the pilgrimage needed to get there. A tunnel takes you into a circular chamber with seats all the way round. The focal point of the round space is a circular hole cut out of the ceiling. The thick ceiling is chiselled down to an edge from the outside, so although the ceiling is very solid, the edge of the hole appears to be very thin. This allows more light in, and enables the viewer to not only watch the sky changing, but also to experience the light changing inside the chamber. At dawn the experience is totally different to that at dusk. As the sun goes down the subtle interior lighting takes over, as gradually it becomes a softly glowing haven from the dark outside world. As Kielder has open access you can stay to watch the light change as the sun sets (try to park at the nearest point to avoid getting lost in the forest afterwards and take a torch), or get up early to watch it as the sun rises. The circular hole in the ceiling is echoed by the round space inside, the circular tunnel, the black circle of gravel in the centre of the floor and, when the sun shines, the bright circle of light which hits the wall. This was certainly one of my favourite pieces.

Belvedere is a fantastic architectural shelter, which looks as if it has just landed from space (it was actually constructed by Softroom). Situated at Benny Shank on the north side of the lake, it can be reached by ferry (in summer) or by walking from Hawkhope car park. The idea was to create something that would blend in with its surroundings but in a new and contemporary way, rather than by using traditional wood or stone. The stainless-steel surface does this by reflecting back its surroundings, and once you have got accustomed to the shock of seeing this peculiar-shaped steel construction perched on the edge of the lake it actually works very well. I wasn't sure about this piece when I saw the picture but loved it in reality. If you go inside, its real function then becomes clear. Inside the shelter are not only benches, but a long thin window offering a curved and panoramic view of the lake. This amazing window is framed at both edges by wings of steel which are part of the outer wall, throwing back the last bit of the view as a reflection. Before you leave, have a look at the strange, futuristic back of the shelter from the outside.

right above: *Belvedere*, by Softroom, 1999. Kielder's first architectural commission, view of the front, with Kielder water behind.
right below: *Belvedere*, by Softroom, 1999. The strange-shaped back of the shelter, with its panoramic window. *Photos by Alison Stace.*

Wave Chamber is perched right on the edge of the lake, where on a windy day waves crash against the rocks. It can be reached by walking from Hawkhope car park. You could be forgiven for thinking that this cone-shaped stone construction is one of Andy Goldsworthy's *Cones*, but it is actually a hut by Chris Drury. It is effectively a camera obscura, and really needs the sun to enable it to work properly, so you may or may not get lucky. The light hits the waves and bounces off onto a mirror, which then directs the light through a small glass lens in the roof of the domed hut onto a stone slab in the floor. Once you are inside the hut with the door shut, you will notice how the darkened interior emphasises the silvery light of the waves, which plays on the floor in mesmerising patterns.

Mirage, by Kisa Kawakami, is accessed from Bakethin Weir, and looks like a strange, slightly messy collection of silver discs suspended from the trees above a series of wooden platforms. The piece intrigued me as I approached it on a cloudy day – but then the sun came out and it was suddenly transformed as the rays of light bounced off the discs, making the treetops, tree trunks and the surrounding forest floor flash and twinkle with thousands of little spots of light. A magical experience.

2a The Angel of the North

Getting there

By road
Located on A1 at the entrance to Gateshead.

From the north (central Gateshead), head south on the Durham road (A167) to Low Fell. Continue through Low Fell until you reach the dual carriageway, then keep going until you reach main roundabout leading to the A1. • Go round the roundabout and take the exit back towards Gateshead South. The Angel site is on your left about 300 yards further on, with parking indicated in the second lay-by.

From the south follow the A1 and A1(M) north until you pass Washington service station. Just past this is jct 65; come off the A1 here. • At the main roundabout take the A167. Continue on for a few hundred yards. The Angel site is on your left, with parking indicated in the second lay-by.

By bus
Buses run to the **Angel of the North** from Gateshead Interchange, Bus Stand K

Buses: 21, 21a, 21b, 724, 728

Overview

The *Angel of the North* by Antony Gormley, which marks the entrance to Gateshead, has become an iconic symbol of the North. Completed and installed in 1998, the *Angel* is Britain's largest sculpture. At 20 m (65 ft) tall and with a wingspan of 54 m (175 ft), it can be seen easily from the A1 as well as from the East Coast train line. It stands on a hilltop, the site of a former colliery, reflecting the industrial history of the area.

It is impossible to appreciate exactly how big the *Angel* is until you stand at its feet. Both awe-inspiring and slightly terrifying, the figure could be either offering protection or demanding compliance, or possibly both, and has immediate connotations with myths and legends from the ancient past.

As one of Gateshead Council's first public commissions, the *Angel* has done much to regenerate the area and open up further opportunities for public-art funding. It also appears to have had a much bigger impact than expected, both on local people and on the general public's attitude towards the area. The *Angel* has won many art awards including the National Art Collection Fund Award for outstanding contribution to the visual arts.

Hartlepool Steel Fabrications constructed the piece for Gormley using Cor-Ten™ weather-resistant steel, plus 32 tonnes of reinforcing steel, and 700 tonnes of concrete poured down into the foundations to anchor the sculpture to solid rock, helping it to cope with winds of more than 100 mph. It is hoped that *The Angel of the North* will last for more than 100 years.

A more recent installation by Antony Gormley is *Another Place*, originally consisting of 100 cast iron figures (about 16 have been moved) which create a dramatic scene along the beach at Crosby, Merseyside. The casts were taken from his own body, a method he often uses. This work was initiated in 2003, and was due to move to New York, but in 2007 was granted permission to remain here.

opposite: *Angel of The North*, by Antony Gormley, 1998. View of the back showing the ribs. *Photo by Alison Stace with permission of Gateshead council.*

2b Art in Gateshead

Information:

Gateshead Tourist Information Centre
The Sage, Gateshead
Hillgate Quay, St Mary's Square,
Gateshead NE8 2GR
Tel: 0191 478 4222
www.gateshead.gov.uk or
www.gateshead.gov.uk/Leisure%20and%20C
ulture/home.aspx

Facilities: The Sage in Gateshead (where you start) has a café and toilets.
Open (visitor centre): Mon-Fri 9am–5pm, Sat 10am–5pm, Sun & bank hols 11am–5pm
Admission: None, though if you come by car you'll need to pay for parking at The Sage – rates depend on how long you will be.
Time needed: 2 hours

Rise and Fall, by Lulu Quinn, 2007. The arch echoes the railway arches behind it, and is lit up gradually through the day. *Photo by Alison Stace, with permission of Gateshead council.*

Getting there

It is important to note that the city of Newcastle and the town of Gateshead are located on opposite sides of the Tyne, though to the untrained eye they appear to merge into one big urban sprawl. A good place to start a tour of sculpture in the area is the Sage, the enormous undulating silver building housing a cafe, toilets and music halls next to the Baltic Mill (centre for contemporary art), located on the Gateshead side of the river.

By road
Take the A167 from the A1, and once you enter Gateshead or Newcastle, head for the bridge and then follow the brown signs to Quayside and The Sage.

By train
The nearest station is Newcastle Central, from where you can either walk (about 20 mins) or take a yellow QuayLink bus (Q1) to The Sage in Gateshead (approx. 5 mins).

above: *Acceleration* (detail), by John Creed, 2005. Cor-Ten™ steel and stainless steel. The whole piece is in two parts and is 7 m long.

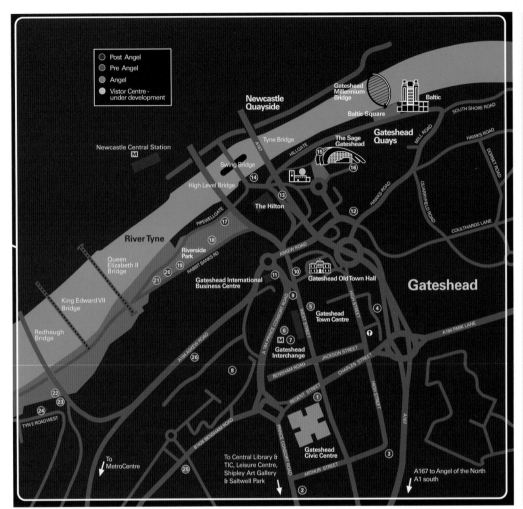

Gateshead Town Centre Art Map

1 **The Family** by Gordon Young, 1991. Cumbrian limestone.
2 **Penny Circus** by Matthew Blackman, 2006. Enamel and concrete.
3 **Threshold** by Lulu Quinn, 2003.
4 **Subways** by David Goard, 2004/05. Printed ceramic tiles.
5 **Sports Day** by Mike Winstone, 1985–6. Painted concrete.
6 **Nocturnal Landscape** by Keith Grant, 1982. Terrazzo mosaic panels.
7 **Opening Line** by Danny Lane, 2004. Steel and glass.
8 **Wind Vane** by Richard Woods, 2001.
9 **Subways** by David Goard, 2004/05. Printed ceramic tiles.
10 **Acceleration** by John Creed, 2005. Cor-Ten™ steel and stainless steel.
11 **Counterpoise** by John Creed, 2005. Stainless steel with coloured spheres.
12 **Blue Beacon** by David Pearl, 2004. Stainless steel and coloured acrylic.
13 **James Hill Monument** by Peter Coates, 2006/07. Blaxter stone.
14 **Orange Beacon** by David Pearl, 2004. Stainless steel and coloured acrylic.
15 **Ribbon of Colour** by Kate Maestri, 2004. Stainless steel and coloured glass.
16 **Star Ceiling** by Jo Fairfax, 2004. Fibre optic cables and tubing.
17 **Rise and Fall** by Lulu Quinn, 2007. Glass and stainless steel.
18 **Cone** by Andy Goldsworthy, 1992. Steel plate.
19 **Rolling Moon** by Colin Rose, 1990. Steel.
20 **Thornbird Railings** by Marcela Livingston, 2005. Iron.
21 **Goats** by Sally Matthews, 1992. Recycled materials.
22 **Once Upon a Time** by Richard Deacon, 1990. Painted mild steel.
23 **Phoenix Cobbles** by Maggy Howarth, 1994. Pebble mosaic.
24 **Entrance Features** by Graeme Hopper, 2005/06. Steel.
25 **Window** by Colin Rose.
26 **Ribbon Railings** by Gateshead Council landscape architects and Alan Dawson Associates, 2002. Galvanised steel.

Finding your way around

Start at the tourist information desk, now located in The Sage. This has copies of the town map showing both Newcastle and Gateshead, and more importantly a booklet called 'The Gateshead Art Map'. Be sure to ask for a copy if it is not visible. The Art Map has information on all the sculptures, and shows you where they are located (see also map above). Although the map does include some street names, it is helped by having the town plan alongside for back-up. There are a lot of sculptures in the Gateshead area, and many of them are scattered and far-flung, involving buses or car journeys to separate areas. The ones shown on this map of the centre are in my opinion some of the best ones, and can also be reached just by walking around central Gateshead. It took me approximately two hours to walk around the ones included on the suggested route (not all are included). Of course, there is no set way, and you can make

Overview

up your own itinerary. The Sage is a convenient place to start from, however, as it is easy to spot, well signposted, has two of the sculptures on its doorstep, and the added advantages of parking, a café and toilets.

The route I took incorporated the following pieces (see corresponding numbers on map): 15, 13, 10, 5, 3, 1 – retrace steps back down West St – 7, 11, 17, 18, 19, 20, 21; then walk back along Pipewellgate to 14 and end at 16 (by entrance to car park).

The nicest area is the Quayside and along the river, and it also has many of the best sculptures, so if you are short of time you could just stick to this route – although you would miss out on several good pieces, including *Threshold*.

Walking around the sculptures at Gateshead is very much an urban experience. Sculptures are scattered all around the town, and while a good many are by the attractive Quayside, many others are located by car parks and shopping centres, or involve crossing busy junctions or large roundabouts, or walking along stretches of rather bleak roadside. However, they are worth the effort.

While many councils have tried to improve their towns with a few sculptures in public places, Gateshead have taken the policy to a new level, commissioning nearly 50 artworks since the early 1980s, including some very exciting, modern pieces. The best-known of these pieces is undoubtedly the *Angel of The North*, beside the main road leading into the town. But the large investment in so many pieces has resulted in a strong body of work sited all over the town. The quayside has also

undergone major renovation, including the recently constructed Sage centre, designed by Norman Foster, a music venue with state-of-the-art concert halls. This imposing building is nevertheless a very welcoming place, with a nice café. Its fantastic architectural qualities can only really be appreciated from the inside, while one of the town's sculptures, the *Ribbon of Colour*, runs through it (see above). Opposite The Sage is the Baltic Centre for Contemporary Art. Converted from a flour mill, this lovely building has changing exhibitions and views across the river from the fifth floor.

left: Map courtesy of Gateshead council.
left: *Ribbon of Colour*, by Kate Maestri, 2004. *Photo by Philip Vile, courtesy of Gateshead Council.*
right: *James Hill Monument*, by Peter Coates, 2007. Carved from Blaxter stone (the same stone as the base of the bridge). *Photo by Alison Stace.*

Things to see

At the Sage Centre you will find the 200 m long *Ribbon of Colour*, designed by Kate Maestri and incorporated into the building by Norman Foster. This consists of coloured panels attached to the balustrade, creating a lovely curving line of changing blues and greens running from the front of the building all the way through the inside. The well-named *Acceleration* (by John Creed) is found on your way into town, dividing the car park from the road. Behind it is the Old Town Hall, housing a temporary cinema (and very nice coffee room). As you walk along West Street you will pass *Sports Day* (by Mike Winstone), an enormous jet-black sculpture depicting the sack race on a school sports day, with animals from Aesop's fable of the tortoise and the hare. It looks incongruous outside the shopping centre but it's still a great piece of accessible art relating to the community. Turn left down Charles Street at the Civic Centre (a red-brick building), then right onto the High Street, and continue along past St Edmund's Church (on your left) until you come to a sharp right bend at the end of the road. In front of you is a short-cut through some trees, with *Threshold* (by Lulu Quinn) standing very tall above the entrance to the path. This sound sculpture was one of my favourites – it is not much to look at; it has to be experienced. Once you have opened the 'invisible gate' by walking through the sculpture along the path (listen for the sound of an enormous creaking door), a random soundtrack is played, a recording from some 300 local people. This can be literally anything – I heard ducks, hundreds of running feet, and a child's birthday party, amongst other things. Then when someone else walks through, the gate 'shuts' (listen for the slamming sound!). Located on a busy walkway, it is constantly being triggered off, turning an uninteresting corner into an active and engaging spot. Well worth the walk.

From here, you can follow the sharp bend and turn right back past the civic centre, where you'll find Gordon Young's chunky figurative stone sculptures of people at various times of life (situated significantly close to the register office). Walk back down West Street, passing on your left the fantastic wave-like sculpture of steel and glass (*Opening Line* by Danny Lane) situated in the middle of Gateshead Interchange (otherwise known as the bus depot). Heading down towards the river you will reach *Acceleration* again and see *Counterpoise* by the same artist, John Creed (away to your left in the car park of the International Business Centre, which is lit up at night). Once you reach the road heading towards the river again, you want to veer left down the side of the buttresses holding up the bridge. After you have passed the *James Hill Monument* marking the life of the fiddle player who lived in Gateshead, turn left (after the blue Beacon) into Pipewellgate (with Buffalo Joe's Bar on the corner) towards the park.

Rise and Fall by Lulu Quinn (also responsible for *Threshold*) is a fabulous archway, installed in 2007, marking the entrance to Riverside Park. Standing 6 m high, it is constructed from stainless steel and turquoise glass, with hundreds of tiny lights inside it. Lights come on gradually throughout the day, until by the evening it is entirely lit up and can be seen across the river. They also light up in a sequence to create the illusion of the arch wobbling, collapsing and rebuilding itself. The park is also home to *Cone* by Andy Goldsworthy. Looking like a giant brown egg through the trees, there is (currently) no path taking you down to it – so you have to settle for glimpsing it through the trees.

After passing *Rolling Moon* further down into the park, if you get back onto the road and turn left you will find Sally Matthews's *Goats* nibbling grass on the embankment. Made from salvaged metal and sited in stages up the embankment, the goats gaze out as if on a terraced Mediterranean hillside.

Return to the Sage on your way out, and be sure to look at the very well-hidden *Star Ceiling*. To find it, head out around the back of the centre to the car-park entrance, a stainless-steel and turquoise-fronted area with lifts up to the top floors. Stand right in front of the lift doors. Now look up – an unexpected, beautiful starry night stares back at you from this secret dark space, its illuminated neon stars suspended on long hanging tubes.

5 Newby Hall Sculpture Park

From Past Memory V, by Richard Jackson. Glass and steel. Exhibited in 2007.

Information:

Newby Hall & Gardens, Estate Office, Newby Hall, Ripon, North Yorkshire, HG4 5AE.
Tel: 0845 450 4068
www.newbyhall.co.uk

Facilities: Toilets, café, educational programmes, stately home, lake, miniature railway, adventure playground
Opening: 1 June–30 Sept
Admission (gardens & sculpture park only): Adult £7.20, OAP £6.20, child £5.80, family £24 or £29. (With admission to the house as well, it is £2–3 extra.)

Getting there

By road
Take the A1(M) to jct 48, then follow A148 towards Dishforth. • Then take the B6265 towards Ripon and follow brown signs. • Newby Hall is signposted off this road, straight ahead along a narrow lane for about 2 miles until you see the gated entrance and stone pillars.

By train
Nearest train station is Harrogate (30 mins by taxi) or York (40 mins by taxi).

Overview

Originally built in the 1690s and enlarged in the 18th century, Newby Hall is a grand stately home (used in ITV's *Mansfield Park*) with lovely gardens. The sculpture trail was started in 2000. Some sculptures are set in the small formal garden area outside the café, and in the grounds immediately around the entrance pavilion, but most can be found on a trail through the woodland area away from the house and gardens. On arrival, you need to park in the extensive car park on the grass, and walk from here up towards the gardens and the entrance; the sculpture park is opposite (the staff will direct you). The sculpture walk takes you through the woodland (very pretty, if a little dark in places, and very welcome on a scorching hot day) and alongside the River Ure.

There were some 58 sculptures on display at the time of visiting: some 15 of these are usually small works located inside the restaurant/gallery area and in the entrance, while the rest can be found outside.

The sculpture park operates very much as an outdoor gallery, and all work is for sale, although this is not the primary objective. The owners' initial idea was to attract visitors, encouraging people to walk in the woodland area and enjoy contemporary art (the owners are great art lovers, and the house has its own very good collection). They try to combine a mixture of established artists (in the past they have shown Anthony Caro, William Pye and Peter Randall Page) with local and new emerging talent. They also try to include about ten new artists every year. Currently, most of the sculptures change every year, but a piece by William Pye was due to become a permanent

fixture. There was a good selection of media at the time of visiting – bronzes, wood, glass, willow and steel, including one kinetic piece – although there were more bronzes than anything else. Obviously, the work changes every year, but Lucinda Compton, who curates the sculpture exhibitions, tries to keep a good mixture. Overall the quality of the sculptures was pretty high, and although most were fairly traditional works, a few were abstract, and some others were stranger, darker pieces with a different perspective. There is also often a display of work in the restaurant/gallery area to accompany the sculptures in the park (such as maquettes and drawings by the artists relating to the sculptures), though in 2007 they broke from this tradition and teamed up with Kentmeer House Gallery to show a selection of paintings. These displays change throughout the summer.

Originally sponsored by Christie's, Newby Hall has been privately funded for the last five years, but this arrangement is due to finish soon. Although the sculpture park does now operate as a successful outdoor gallery, from 2008 onwards the owners will be looking for new sponsorship.

far left: *Pair of Horses*, by Emma Stothard. Steel wire and willow. Exhibited in 2007.
left: *Generations*, by Stuart Brett. Stone and metal. Exhibited in 2007.
right: *The Fall of Adam and Eve* (detail), by Reece Ingram. Sweet-chestnut wood. Exhibited in 2007.

Finding your way around

Leaflets for the sculpture park are available at the entrance pavilion, and also by the entrance to the sculpture park itself in a container on the wall. The leaflet has a map with numbered works on it, and all sculptures have a little plaque bearing their title and maker's name. Allow 30–45 minutes for the walk through the woodland, depending on your speed.

Things to see

The work at Newby Hall changes annually, but, to give a broad outline, 2007 offered a good selection of animal forms, from the quiet and thoughtful (if slightly arrogant) hare by Nicola Toms, to Guy Portelli's lovely giant dragonfly with glass mosaic wings which sparkled mesmerically in the sun, to the superb life-size pair of horses by Emma Stothard (created from willow and wire, a great combination of media).

On a conceptual level there was *Outlook* by Gillian Brent, which the leaflet described as 'a playful comment on Georgian architecture', based on the idea of the servants in the attic, and how different their view of life outside would have been from those high tiny windows when compared with that of their owners through the large drawing-room windows. These free-standing metal windows on poles were placed at different heights and angles, framing small sections of land or sky and describing the invisible form of the house.

The best of the abstract works included *Bronze Dreaming Stone* by Peter Randall-Page (his first large-scale bronze) and two others both made by Deirdre Hubbard – a *Hybrid Bird*, and *Wingless Pair*, a pair of organically shaped seeds offering a fabulous range of curves in both their shapes and the spaces in between the pair – in a bronze that positively glowed in the sun.

4 Yorkshire Sculpture Park

Information:

Yorkshire Sculpture Park,
West Bretton, Wakefield, WF4 4LG.
Tel: 01924 830579
Web: www.ysp.co.uk

Facilities: Café, toilets, educational pro-
grammes.
Open: Summer: 26 March–30 Oct
grounds & centre 10am–6pm,
Longside gallery 11am–3pm.
Winter: 30 Oct–25 March
grounds & centre, 10am–5pm.
Closed: 23–25 Dec
Admission: free (donations), (car park: £4)

Getting there

By road
Exit 38 off the M1, follow brown heritage
signs to YSP on the A637, then turn off at
the first roundabout (signposted).

By train
Wakefield Westgate station (about 2 hours
from London King's Cross), and approx.
15 mins by taxi.

One and Other, by Antony Gormley, 2000. Cast
iron. *Photo by Jonty Wilde, courtesy of Yorkshire
Sculpture Park.*

Overview

The first impression of the Yorkshire Sculpture Park that greets you on arrival (apart from the state-of-the-art angular visitor centre designed by Feilden Clegg Bradley, with its long path of names leading to the door), is the hilarious juxtaposition of sheep and grass with enormous bronze sculptures by Henry Moore. Fluffy Yorkshire sheep nibble around the base of the plinths on which these giant sculptures stand. Yorkshire Sculpture Park is one of the biggest and most established of the sculpture parks. The standard of sculpture is very high, with pieces by many internationally recognised artists from the last 100 years, including Henry Moore, Anthony Gormley, Elisabeth Frink, David Nash and Barbara Hepworth. As such it is a great place to get an instant overview of the development of British sculpture since the first part of the 20th century. The Henry Moore section that greets you on arrival is set out across a wide hillside, with a sweeping view down towards a river. Work by Barbara Hepworth is also shown on a regular basis. The visitor centre has a large gallery downstairs, with changing exhibitions which sometimes spill out into the formal gardens below. The Longside Gallery at the opposite end of the park also houses exhibitions and in any case is worth the walk, given the interesting sculptures along the way. Check the website or ask at the main centre reception what is showing – be warned, though, that the Longside Gallery does not have a café, so you may want to have lunch before setting off for the other side (approximately a 30–40 minute walk).

A more recent addition to YSP is the new *Skyspace*, designed by James Turrell. This work has been in progress since 1993 and finally opened in 2007. Turrell has worked with concepts of light and space for 40 years, and this *Skyspace* is only the second one he has built in this country (the first is at Kielder Water, see pp.15–16). The *Skyspace* has been constructed within the Deer Shelter – an 18th-century construction. If you go to YSP you simply have to go and experience this amazing space (see p.30). It is relatively near the visitor centre, so if you are short of time you should still be able to visit it.

YSP was established 30 years ago for the public to enjoy and has changed radically from its beginnings in a small wooden hut. The grounds were part of an estate that was landscaped over 200 years ago, but was split up in the 1940s before being brought back together by the sculpture park in recent years. The Underground Gallery, following the building of the impressive visitor centre, was also designed by architects Feilden Clegg Bradley, and was shortlisted for the 2006 Gulbenkian Prize.

Reclining Figure Arch Leg, by Henry Moore, 1969–70. On loan from the Henry Moore Foundation, this is the first sculpture to greet you. *Photo by Jonty Wilde, courtesy of Yorkshire Sculpture Park.*

Getting around

The park is divided up into sections that have been colour-coded in the comprehensive map provided to aid navigation around the park. The full guide comes in colour-coded leaflets corresponding to the map (which fold up into a neat holder that you can wear around your neck), giving a summary of each artist's works.

The park has a veritable feast of sculptures, and trying to see everything is quite exhausting. This is partly because there is so much here, and partly because significant sculptures are scattered throughout the various areas, as well as across the 1 ¼ mile (2 km) stretch of fields and grounds between the visitor centre and the Longside Gallery at the opposite end. Our visit lasted five hours, which included looking at everything, a half-hour lunch stop at the very pleasant café, as well as walking across to the Longside Gallery. The map suggests routes to follow, and gives a rough idea of how long it will take. From experience, I would recommend covering the smaller, upper areas first and having lunch, before heading over to the caféless Longside Gallery. If you feel it is all too much, you could simply target specific areas instead.

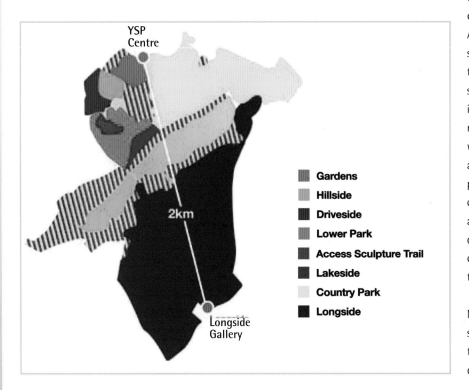

YSP
Centre

2km

Longside
Gallery

- Gardens
- Hillside
- Driveside
- Lower Park
- Access Sculpture Trail
- Lakeside
- Country Park
- Longside

Things to see

As the YSP leaflet puts it, James Turrell's work 'is about light, but more importantly it is light', and one sculpture you should definitely see when coming here is Turrell's new *Skyspace* in the Deer Shelter. This shrine to light is an almost spiritual experience, which on its own makes the trip to YSP worthwhile. The entrance, which is hidden behind the three arches of the old deer shelter, consists of a doorway like that of an ancient Egyptian tomb. It leads into a secret chamber entirely lined by stone seats with very high backs. Along the top of the backs is very subdued lighting, while the whole room slopes gently outwards and upwards towards the ceiling, encouraging you to lean back and look up. Above you, cut out of the ceiling, is a perfect square that appears to be as thin as a line (although it is actually very solid). The cut-out square reveals the ever-changing sky, allowing light to fill the room, which changes dramatically or very subtly depending on the weather conditions outside. The space has an almost monastic feel. One of the greatest pleasures the piece offers is to watch the light change in the *Skyspace* throughout the day, and especially as the sun comes up or goes down – although, given the opening and closing times at YSP, that is harder to do here than with the *Skyspace* at Kielder Water.

Most of the routes suggested by the map start with the Gardens Zone, which includes the Underground Gallery and the formal gardens and terrace, usually home to changing exhibitions. Many of Elisabeth Frink's sculptures were being moved here together in 2007, to the area just below the formal gardens.

The Hillside Zone is home to Jonathan Borofsky's *Molecule Man 1+1+1*. You can see right through this huge, spacious sculpture due to all the holes cut out of it (representing the molecules). The two enormous, flat cut-out figures are joined to each other around a central axis, and appear to be arguing and running through or at each other. This sculpture is presumably intended to represent the state of man in general.

Sheep, by Sophie Ryder, 1988. Galvanised wire. *Photo courtesy of Yorkshire Sculpture Park.*

Barbara Hepworth's work is also featured on this hillside (although pieces on display may change). Hepworth and Henry Moore were contemporaries and had a great deal of influence on the development of modernist sculpture. She spent most of her life in St Ives in Cornwall, where her home and gardens have been open to the public for many years (see p.144). One of few artists at this time to create enormous pieces specifically for the outdoors, the curved, organic forms of her work make it particularly suited to being displayed in a landscape setting. One piece in this vein is *Curved Reclining Form* (Rosewall), made from Nebrasina stone, which may represent the land seen from Rosewall Rock, where she went to draw. *Two Forms (Divided Circle)* shows Hepworth's interest in abstract shapes

and their relationship to each other. By placing circles within a circle, and dividing it, the viewer is made to think about the elemental shapes, the universe split, and the gap that invites the viewer to peer between or enter, and which draws the viewer in towards these elemental forces. As with *Squares with Two Circles*, the shapes created by the holes and the spaces are as important as the shapes created by the solid sculpture.

Driveside Zone (next to Hillside) is a small area that could be easy to miss – but don't, as among others (including works by David Nash) it is home to some fantastic sculptures in bronze by Elisabeth Frink, another internationally renowned 20th-century British artist. Frink was committed to figurative

sculpture, and worked from themes linked to the Second World War concerning both the atrocities committed and the strength of those caught up in it. *Running Man* (most of her figures are male) appears thin and wiry, like someone who has struggled to survive, and wears a serious, intense look as he runs. Frink and Hepworth would build an armature and cover it in plaster, into which they carved directly, creating a model the same size as the final bronze piece which was cast from it. This means that the marks you see on Frink's sculptures are the marks she made herself. *Sitting Man II*, in contrast to *Running Man*, looks like a warrior, heavily muscled and with a sinister-looking painted face that is both fascinating

above: *Promenade* by Anthony Caro.
opposite: *Outclosure* by Andy Goldsworthy, 2007. *Photo by Jonty Wilde, photos courtesy of Yorkshire Sculpture Park.*

and frightening. Be sure also to see the *Water Buffalo* which gaze at each other and capture the heavy-set essence of beast. Some of her work was sited just below the formal gardens – check on arrival as pieces get moved around.

There is a great deal to see in the Lower Park Zone, but my three favourites in this area are *The Arkville Minotaur* (Michael Ayrton), *Large Nijinski Hare on Anvil Point* (Barry Flanagan) and the *Stags* and *Sheep* (Sophie Ryder). Barry Flanagan's irreverent dancing hare on top of a giant anvil actually made me gasp at its bizarre size and subject matter (see also Roche Court and Chatsworth). Sophie Ryder's animals are made from bundles of galvanised wire (in my opinion a fantastically expressive and under-utilised medium) joined to a steel armature. On arriving at YSP you encounter the Country Park Zone (yellow), a hillside covered in sculptures by Henry Moore. It is unusual to find so much of his work in one place (other than at

the Henry Moore Foundation or specific exhibitions) so it is well worth taking a browse amongst the sheep to see it. It is important to mention here that the Henry Moore collection is one of the most mobile in the country, so sculptures at YSP are on loan from the Foundation but are often sent out to other exhibitions. However, though the inventory of pieces does change, there are always a few key works to see. One of these is the *Draped Seated Woman* (1957–58). This piece is more representative than much of his work, though the exaggerated torso and fabric is clearly what interested Moore. Gazing regally down the hill, this figure commands respect and attention while seated somewhat awkwardly on her stair-shaped plinth.

Reclining Figure Arch Leg is a somewhat bizarre and disjointed sculpture – literally disjointed, as the enlarged, elongated arched leg has been split off from the rest of the body,

making the viewer examine the piece again and look at the body in a different way. Moore's approach to the figure means that the viewer is almost forced to examine each part of the body separately, seeing it as a series of shapes creating spaces with each position, rather than as biological anatomy. His work became more abstract as he grew older, as you can see from *Bunched* (1985), which still captures the suggestion of a body while being totally pared down to what he saw as its essential form. *Large Two Forms* are two enormous organic-shaped pieces that relate to each other, and create amazing shapes as you walk around them. Like many of his two-piece forms, the shapes and the view changes dramatically from each angle, another reason he felt his work needed to be placed outdoors where people could view them through the full 360 degrees. (For more information about Henry Moore see pp. 89–95.)

Lakeside Zone is home to Anthony Caro's enormous angular quasi-architectural steel sculptures, and Sol LeWitt's mathematical breeze-block construction. Anthony Caro was a contemporary of Moore's and was one of the first artists to do away with the plinth. A seemingly simple and unremarkable concept by today's standards, it was shocking and revolutionary at the time. It brings the art down to the viewer's level, inviting a more direct relationship with the piece, and also making us look around at other everyday objects and ask, 'What is art?'

Longside Zone covers the whole area on the other side of the lake. A large field lies between the lake and the Longside Gallery, and a few key sculptures can be seen along the way. One of these is Antony Gormley's stunning *One and Other*, whose site the artist chose very carefully. Gormley always works on figurative pieces, often using casts

of his own body. Balanced on top of a huge tree stump this figure towers over the path and is visible from some distance away. This is both an awe-inspiring and frustrating experience, as you want to get up close for a proper look, but the piece stands tantalisingly out of reach. Made from cast iron, the work's intense orange colour comes from the natural rusting of the metal.

On the way to Longside Gallery are Andy Goldsworthy's new installations. These are the permanent remainders (*Hanging Trees* is permanent and *Outclosure* is also possibly staying) of the enormous exhibition of his work at YSP in 2007. Now one of the foremost contemporary land artists, Goldsworthy first created work here in 1983, and constructed these new pieces for the 30th anniversary of the sculpture park. Much of his work deals with issues concerning land – in particular ownership and accessibility. *Hanging Trees* has been deliberately constructed within the wall of the ha-ha on Oxley Bank. The ha-ha was a land construct or 'screen' often used by large stately homes, consisting of an embankment of earth which hid the stone walls so that divisions in the land were not visible from the house – the estate grounds then appeared to blend in with the surrounding land and fields, suggesting that the estate extended as far as the eye could see. Goldsworthy undermines this construct by forcing you to get up close and look at the divisions. His work forces the viewer to engage with the land more directly. It also works to draw visitors away from the 'safety' of the gallery into the land.

The tree trunks Goldsworthy has built into and within the boxed confines of the wall are almost like giant specimens in cases. These specimens, however, are very much bound into their boxes. It is not clear whether the tree is trapped by the wall, or somehow supporting it. The two are intertwined. As the YSP leaflet states, these

above: *Sitting Man* by Elisabeth Frink, 1986. Bronze. *Photo by Jonty Wilde, courtesy of Yorkshire Sculpture Park.*
opposite: *Terris Novalis* by Tony Cragg (with cyclists), 1994/5. Located on the Consett to Sunderland cycle route. *Photo courtesy of Cheatle/ Sustrans.*

pieces evoke the idea of mountains which 'slowly crumble when they are cleared of trees'. The relationship between wood and stone is therefore very fragile and complex – as it is between man and nature.

Outclosure, located in a circular cluster of trees, called Round Wood, is found at the end of Oxley Bank walk near Longside Gallery. This perfectly enclosed dry-stone wall is too high to see over and has no gaps or windows anywhere. I walked all round it twice, looking for a way in. The wall hides a secret internal space. It is very frustrating to be kept out. This, however, is the point.

Basket No.7. Oxley Bank, on loan to YSP since 2004, is a two-storey steel building situated on a hill on the way to the Longside Gallery. Designed by German collaborative artists Winter and Hörbelt, this piece, made of mesh, is quite disconcerting. It appears sometimes solid and sometimes transparent, and is hard to get a fix on until you get right up close. Inside is a kind of maze opening out into rooms, but also offering views through the walls of the landscape beyond. It offers both a fantastic and unsettling experience at the same time. You can see not only the trees and the field beyond, but also the sky above and the room beneath you all at once.

Other Places of Interest
4 Consett to Sunderland

Information:

Sustrans (Head Office)
National Cycle Network Centre, 2 Cathedral
Square, College Green, Bristol, BS1 5DD.
Tel: 0845 113 0065
www.sustrans.org.uk

Getting There

By road or train
To start at Consett, take A1(M) and come
off at jct 63 onto A693, then A692 to Consett. **To start at Sunderland**, from A1(M)
take jctn 65 onto A1231 to Sunderland.
Route starts at Roker Pier promenade by
marina. **By train**, Sunderland station then
10 mins by bicycle.

By bicycle (or on foot)
The route to Sunderland can be picked up
at Consett where the B6308 meets the
A692. The route from Consett goes over
the bridge, crossing the B692, and then
continues further on, on the right-hand side
of the A693 briefly, before turning left onto
the railway path. The route goes through
Stanley, (past the Beamish Open Air Museum), Pelton, Rickleton, past Washington
Arts Centre, through Fatfield, skirts South
Hylton and then follows the River Wear to
Sunderland, ending on the promenade. At
Sunderland stay on the left-hand side of
the river until you reach the marina and
promenade by Roker Pier. Detailed maps
of the route can be obtained from Sustrans.

The North-east

Overview

This is one of the routes set up by Sustrans as a cycle route (although it can be walked) and is part of a much larger one (the Sea to Sea Cycle route). The whole sea-to-sea route goes from White-haven or Workington to Sunderland or Newcastle. We are just looking at a small stretch of it though (cycle route No.7), which has some fantastic art-works along it, most of these (1–14) were com-missioned by Sustrans (apart from the Andy Goldsworthy), and which includes work by Tony Cragg, Richard Harris, Andy Goldsworthy, Ken Tur-nell, David Kemp and John Downie amongst oth-ers. The *Jolly Drover's Maze* by Goldsworthy is a beautifully constructed maze built on the site of a former colliery, with the cycle path weaving its way through. From Consett to Sunderland is 24 miles, but there is an alternative way back for those feeling adventurous which takes 39 miles going through Gateshead and Newcastle, which passes some other fantastic sculptures (No.16 *Conversation Piece* and No.14 *Shadows in Another Light*) and also skirts past some of the artwork found in Gateshead (see pp.20–24). Most of the route is off-road, but there are parts that follow roads through towns, and occasionally you need to make small detours to see artworks. You may also need to book a B&B to break up the journey, unless you are a particularly fit and speedy cyclist.

top right: *Lambton Worm,* by Andy Goldsworthy, c.1990, in snow. *Photo courtesy of S. Shorthouse/Sustrans.*
bottom: *The Old Transformers,* by David Kemp, c.1991. *Photo courtesy of Nicola Jones/Sustrans.*
left: *King Coal,* by David Kemp, 1992/3. *Photo cour-tesy of Nicola Jones/Sustrans.*

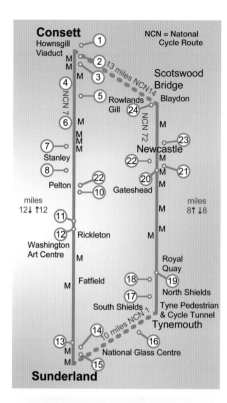

Consett
Hownsgill Viaduct
① 1
NCN = Natonal Cycle Route
M M
② 2
M
③ 3
13 miles NCN14
Scotswood Bridge
④ 4
NCN 7
⑤ 5
Rowlands Gill
Blaydon
② 24
⑥ 6
M
NCN 72
M
⑦ 7
Stanley
M M M
② 23
Newcastle
② 22
M
⑧ 8
② 21
② 22
② 20
M
Pelton
② 10
Gateshead
miles
12↓ ↑12
M
miles
8↑ ↓8
① 11
① 12
Rickleton
Washington Art Centre
M
M
Royal Quay
Fatfield
① 18
① 19
M
North Shields
① 17
South Shields
Tyne Pedestrian & Cycle Tunnel
Tynemouth
10 miles NCN 1
① 14
① 16
① 13
M
National Glass Centre
M
① 15
Sunderland

1 **Hot Metal Carriage** from former Consett Steelworks
2 **Terris Novalis** by Tony Cragg
3 **Entrance to Maze** by Graeme Hopper
4 **Jolly Drover's Maze** by Andy Goldsworthy
5 **Old Transformers** by David Kemp
6 **Kyo Undercurrent** by Richard Harris
7 **Flower Mine** by Ken Turnell
8 **Beamish Shorthorns** by Sally Matthews
9 **The Celestial Railroad** by John Downie
10 **King Coal** by David Kemp
11 **Lambton Earthwork** by Andy Goldsworthy
12 **Sleeper Seats** by Liz Walmesley and Jim Partridge
13 **Sunderland Enterprise Park Stone Carvings** by Colin Wilbourn
14 **St Peter's Riverside Sculpture Project** by Colin Wilbourn, Karl Fisher, Craig Knowles, Chaz Brenchley and others
15 **Ambit** by Alison Wilding
16 **Conversation Piece** by Juan Muñoz
17 **Fish Quay Bollards and Fencing** by Northern Freeform
18 **Tyne Anew** by Mark Di Suvero
19 **Rugged Landscape and Waterfalls** (Redburn Dene & Chirton Dene) by Tyne & Wear Development Corp.
20 **Gateshead Millenium Bridge** by Wilkinson and Eyre
21 **Blacksmith's Needle** by British Association of Blacksmith Artists (on Newcastle Quayside)
22 **Rolling Moon** by Colin Rose (in Gateshead Riverside Sculpture Park)
23 **Spheres** by Richard Cole (Newcastle Business Park)
24 **Derwent Walk Express** by Andy Frost

Map courtesy of Sustrans and Joe Knight.

The North-west

- Cumbria • Lancashire • Greater Manchester
- Merseyside

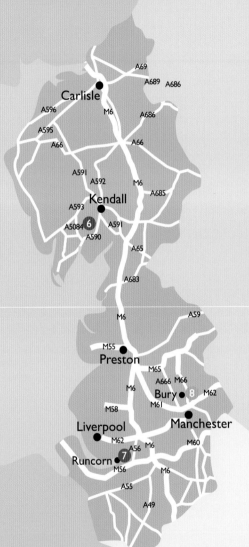

A69
A689 A686
Carlisle
A596
M6
A686
A595
A66
A66
A591
A592
M6
A685
Kendall
A593
A5084 6 A591
A590
A65
A683
M6
A59
M55
Preston
M65
A666 M66
M6
Bury 8 M62
M58
M61
Liverpool
Manchester
M62
M60
Runcorn 7 A56 M6
M56
M6
A55
A49

6 Grizedale Forest Park
7 Norton Priory Sculpture Trail

Other Places of Interest
8 Irwell Sculpture Trail
9 Fred Festival/Art Invasion
(not on map)

6 Grizedale Forest Park

Information:

Hawkshead, Ambleside, Cumbria, LA22 OOJ.
Tel: 0845 3673787
www. forestry.gov.uk/grizedale

Cross Lakes Shuttle
Tel: 01539 445161
www.lakedistrict.gov.uk/index/enjoying/trav-elandtransport/cross_lakes_shuttle.htm

Facilities: Toilet, café, book & gift shop (being refurbished).
Open: seven days a week, all year, but check for Christmas, New Year and January opening.
Café open: daily 10am–5pm (summer), 10am–4pm (winter).
Admission: Free (car park £3)
Time needed: 3 days

Between Elephants, by Iraida Cano, 1995. Located on the Silurian Way. *Photo by Julie Coldwell, courtesy of Grizedale Park.*

Getting there

By road

Grizedale Forest Park is pretty remote. Currently, going by road is the easiest option.
• To avoid the ferry, take the M6 to Jct 36, then the A590 towards Kendal and Windermere. • The A590 runs out soon after, becoming the A591, follow this up to Ambleside. • At Ambleside follow signs for Clappersgate and the A593, then turn left shortly afterwards onto B5286 into the forest, and follow signs to Hawkshead (B5285). • At Hawkshead turn left and follow signs to Grizedale Forest, and head for the central visitors centre.

By boat

If you are travelling around the Lakes, the Cross Lakes Shuttle boat covers many of the tourist/lake areas and runs from April to October (see contact details on p.39). It is possible to take the train to Windermere, then a bus to Bowness on Windermere, and from there catch the Cross Lakes Shuttle. A new park-and-ride scheme is to be put into operation but no details were available at time of going to press.

right: *Habitat* by Richard Caink, 1994. Located on the east side of the forest. *Photo by Julie Coldwell, courtesy of Grizedale Park.*
far right: *Windthrust,* by Jony Easterby, 1996. Located in the east side of the forest, along Bogle Crag Trail. *Photo by Julie Coldwell, courtesy of Grizedale Park.*

Overview

Grizedale Forest Sculpture Park is one of the largest of the sculpture parks, and its management has now been taken over by the Forestry Commission. In the 1990s the focus of the Forestry Commission broadened to include 'managing forests for the sustainable production of timber, for recreation, conservation and the landscape'.

Grizedale's vast size and the sheer quantity and variety of trails means that, apart from the easier routes around the centre, you are

often walking quite far between sculptures. It's as much about the land and forest as about the sculpture. The standard of artwork may not always reach the same consistently high level, but what it lacks occasionally in the quality of sculpture it certainly makes up

for in terms of views and walking. Of course, the size of the forest and the quantity of pieces – more than 80 sculptures spread over an area of 6047 acres – makes it hard to maintain high standards, but there are still some fantastic pieces here. The visitor centre, with café, toilets and gift/bookshop, is currently being refurbished.

The sculptures in the park vary enormously. Some are starting to weather severely: as well as the landscape being some of the most dramatic of the sculpture parks, Grizedale is also one of the oldest, with some pieces having been here now for 26 years. The weathering of a piece will gradually alter its appearance, with changes becoming part of the sculpture, often softening it so that it harmonises ever more closely with the landscape; occasionally, however, the deterioration can leave a sculpture looking jaded and forlorn. In 2007 some of the older sculptures to have suffered this fate were removed. However, some pieces have benefited from the ageing process, such as *Some Fern* by Kerry Morrison, an enormous wooden fern-like carving that increasingly blends in with the bracken around it, despite its size. This is part of the charm of Grizedale – sculptures change with the landscape. Sculptures which once stood out baldly in a clearing have been overtaken by the forest and are now hidden from view, making a lovely surprise when stumbled across. It's like a giant game of buried treasure – just be sure to take the map.

Finding your way around

The beauty of the paths and trails through the forest is that they often cut across each other, so a walk can be tailored as you go, depending on the weather, the length required or specific sculptures of interest. The visitor centre provides maps with trails graded as to length and difficulty, from 1 mile up to 10 miles – don't even think about setting off without one! One of the longer trails, the 'Silurian Way', described as 'strenuous', was supposedly 10 miles, and is estimated to take five hours to complete. Of course, that doesn't allow for the weather, lunch stops, short sideways expeditions to locate sculptures hidden amongst the trees, or the occasional small detour due to a lapse in map reading. We pruned about a mile and a half off our walk by taking shortcuts, but still managed to use up five hours. If you are following a longer route such as this, be sure to take a packed lunch, as the only café is back at the start by the visitor centre. If you are relatively local, or have the time, the size of Grizedale Forest means that you could easily spend about three days here and just about see everything.

Things to see

A misleading concept in the case of Grizedale, as you are unlikely to be able to see everything in one visit. As the forest is managed by the Forestry Commission for the enjoyment of the public, sculptures here are not for sale. This means that pieces which once looked fabulous may now look a little worn. However, there are some fantastic sculptures here, some of the newer pieces under a scheme intending to display sculptures for short periods (i.e. a year or two). It is well worth finding Andy Goldsworthy's *Taking a Wall for a Walk* (sculpture no. 32)

below: *Taking a Wall for a Walk* by Andy Goldsworthy, 1990. Located on the High Bowkerstead Trail. *Photo courtesy of Grizedale Arts.*
right: *An Enlightened Stand* by Donald Urquhart, 1999. Located on the Silurian Way. *Photo by Alison Stace, by permission of Grizedale Forest Park.*

as it weaves in and out of the trees, vaguely reminiscent of Gaudí's mosaic bench in the Gaudí Park, Barcelona. This has now crumbled somewhat from its original tidy state since some trees fell on it, but, as the artist has pointed out, this is the nature of the piece in its outdoor location. Goldsworthy has asked that it be left to crumble slowly, rather than being rebuilt, as some of the trees it wound around are no longer there.

The two *Ancient Forester* sculptures by David Kemp are very tall and melancholy wood carvings, each one looking as though it was carved from a single tree. One is hard to miss, located in the car park by the visitor centre. *Habitat* by Richard Caink is a bizarrely relocated front room, complete with TV, lampshade and armchair, and makes you re-think the idea of urban comfort as being the

norm. Iraido Cano's *Between Elephants* was quite hard to locate, despite its size, and eventually we stumbled across it while looking for something else – but it was impressive once found.

Some of the more unusual sculptures included *You Make Me Feel Mighty Real*, by Fat, which looked totally out of place in the forest. The outside of this modern-looking structure is covered with tiny squares which move and shimmer in the wind, making it look like a huge building-shaped disco mirror ball. *After the Rain/Flood* by David Stewart is an eerie group of what looks like bits of building and columns, half-buried, scattered through a patch of forest, like the remains of a civilisation after the deluge has subsided. Let's hope it isn't a glimpse of the future after global warming. Finally, one of my favourite pieces was *An Enlightened Stand* by Donald Urquhart, a huge flat white cut-out that stands amongst the trees, looking as if they have grown up through it. It took me a while to realise that the shadows from the trees are not real – they are also cut-outs. As site-specific installations go, I think this works superbly – it held me spellbound for some time. Definitely worth the hike.

left: *Light Column,* by Charles Bray, 1994. Located on the east side of the forest.
opposite: *Kitty's Gate*, designed by Daine Gorvin and constructed in wrought iron by Tony Doughty, 1988. Located at Norton Priory. *Photo by Alison Stace, by permission of Norton Priory Trust.*

7 Norton Priory Sculpture Trail

Information:

The Norton Priory Museum Trust, Norton Priory Museum & Gardens, Tudor Road, Manor Park, Runcorn, Cheshire, WA7 1SX.
Telephone: 01928 569895
www.nortonpriory.org

Facilities: Café, toilets, educational programmes, museum.
Open: April–Oct (Mon–Fri 12–5pm, Sat & Sun 12–6pm), Nov–March (daily 12–4pm); closed 24–26 Dec & 1 Jan.
Admission: Adults £4.95, concessions & kids (aged 5–15): £3.50, under 5s: free, family: £12.75.
Time needed: 2–2½ hours

Getting there

By road

• Take M6 to Jct 20, then take M56 towards Runcorn and Chester. • Come off at Jct 11 on M56, take A56 heading east at round-about. • Turn left onto A558, and go straight over at roundabout immediately after. • Follow brown signposts to Norton Priory at the next series of roundabouts.

By bicycle

A cycle path runs right through this site from Runcorn towards Sandymoor, and new cycle paths are being developed in the area.

By train

Runcorn station, then a 10-minute taxi ride (or a 3-mile walk).

Overview

Norton Priory Sculpture Trail is situated in the grounds of a ruined monastery. A very atmospheric place, the remains of the undercroft are still in evidence. The sculpture is sited in the extensive gardens. Ask at reception for the sculpture-trail folder, which has information on all the pieces and can be taken round with you. The whole place is geared towards education, and there are folders of information on everything here – history, trees, buildings, etc. The artwork here has all been supported by various public and private bodies, and has been an ongoing project for the last 20 years or so.

The site is divided by the A558, but you cross from one side to the other by means of a bridge above the traffic. Despite this busy road, the priory is a surprisingly calm and well-hidden retreat. The gardens are very pretty. On one half of the site a small wood full of rhododendrons has little paths and old water courses running through it, while the other half comprises the attractive and surprisingly large (2½ acres) Georgian walled garden, with a variety of flowers as well as space for a pagoda, a walled walkway and a croquet lawn.

The work at Norton Priory is not the most amazing sculpture you will ever see, but it is set in very attractive surroundings, which include a couple of well-designed and well-made gates (see p.45). Make sure you go into the glass-encased room in the main reception to see the enormous (3.5m tall)

sculpture of St Christopher, by an unknown artist from the late 1300s. The small wooded area by the ruins has numerous twisting paths to explore, while next to the walled garden is an orchard. Combine the sculpture and the gardens with the history of the place, and it makes for an interesting day out.

left: *Planthead*, by Diane Gorvin, 1989. Modelled in clay, then cast in cement fondue and painted with acrylics. *Image courtesy of Norton Priory Trust.*
right: *Walled Garden Mosaic* by Hannah Mudd, 1982 (detail). This mosaic is built into the wall in a far corner of the walled garden. The faces are children's faces which have been cast in plaster and then a mould taken in clay. *Photo by Alison Stace, by permission of Norton Priory Trust.*

Finding your way around

Entrance into the gardens and wood is through the museum. There are a number of ways you can navigate the site. There is a leaflet at the desk with a very good line drawing of the paths and garden areas, with triangles marking out the location of sculptures. However, this doesn't tell you what they are. Inside the sculpture-trail folder is a set of comprehensive information sheets on each of the works, and also another map with numbers which correlate to the printed sheets. The numbers are in sequence so as to take you round all the areas. The grounds cover a total of 38 acres (though a good chunk of this is just orchard), so allow between 2 and 2½ hrs to see all the sculpture.

Things to see

Don't leave without sticking your head inside the screened-off glass room in reception. It is hard to see through because of all the reflections, but inside is a huge original statue of St Christopher, dating back to the end of the 14th century. By the new herb garden, the unnervingly simple and serene expression of the *Kneeling Monk*, by Tom Dagnall, was quite compelling. wasn't sure that I liked the figure,

but I did think it captured the history of the place really well. The monk is shown kneeling (trowel in hand) by the herb garden. The artist aimed to connect the 'timeless internal world of the sculpture with the real world of the herb garden and priory' (Tom Dagnall, 1987), in other words linking the internal spiritual world with the physical gardening the monks had to do.

Strangely, one artist is responsible for several pieces of work here, all of which I thought stood out. Set near to a thriving patch of giant leaves (gunnera) *Planthead* (by Diane Gorvin) is located amongst rhododendron bushes. The enormous gunnera leaves look quite surreal, and so does the large morphing woman's head: her calm and beautiful face is framed by the folds of a plant form where you would normally expect to find hair. The head has been located so that the back of it faces outwards – possibly to display the strange, plant-like form – you now have to squeeze in front of the bushes to see her face properly.

Diane Gorvin was also the designer of the two fabulous gates at the walled garden. One is a *Tree of Life*, inspired by a coffin lid from the museum. It represents both physical and spiritual growth and is the first gate to the walled garden (although this is not the entrance). Through its waving branches you can see the garden flourishing. My favourite, though, was *Kitty's Gate*, inspired by a story about a maid from the mansion who had drowned herself in the pond nearby (then named Kitty's Pit). It was rumoured that she was pregnant – a not uncommon occurrence in housemaids, who were often seduced, coerced or forced by the master of the house, who would then generally deny all knowledge. The gate depicts her out on a windy day and captures her despair.

above: *The Kneeling Monk* by Tom Dagnall, 1987. *Photo by Alison Stace, by permission of Norton Priory Trust.*

Other Places of Interest
8 Irwell Sculpture Trail

Untitled, by Ulrich Rückriem, 1999. Porrino granite. Located in Outwood, Radcliffe. *Photo courtesy of Tony Trehy, Arts & Museums Manager, Bury.*

Information:

Bury Tourist Information Centre, Market Street, Bury, Greater Manchester, BL9 0BW. (**Open:** Mon–Fri 9.30am–5pm, Sat 10am–4pm) Tel: 0161 253 5111

OR Clifton Country Park Visitor Centre, Clifton House Road, Clifton, Salford M27 6NG (**Open:** mon–tue 1–5pm, wed–sun 9.30–5pm) Tel: 0161 793 4219

www.irwellsculpturetrail.co.uk

East Lancashire Railway (steam train) Tel: 0161 764 7790 www.east-lancs-rly.co.uk

Facilities: There are toilets and a café (in summer) at Burrs Country Park, otherwise use public facilities.
Open: All year
Admission: Free
Time needed: 1 day

Getting there

This is an unusual trail, which, being 30 miles long, covers a huge area and takes in several small towns. This summary will concentrate on a small section covering Radcliffe, Bury and Ramsbottom. I would suggest starting in Clifton Country Park (which is a short detour off the main trail but is marked on OS maps), and walking towards Radcliffe and Bury. Alternatively, start from either Burrs Country Park (near Bury), which has parking and facilities, or Bury itself (which has a large car park right next to the steam train station), and walk up to Ramsbottom.

Take the M60 to jct 17, and follow the A56 to Bury (the steam train starts here). [Parking in Bury: Find Bolton St and turn into the steep car park by the steam train station. Come back onto Bolton St on foot and turn left, head to the end of the road, cross Carlyle St and go into the subway – you are now on leaflet 6 of the Bury-to-Burrs section of the written instructions.] For Burrs Country Park, once you arrive in Bury on the A56, turn left (from the south) or right (from the north) onto the A58 towards Ramsbottom, and follow the brown signs to Burrs Country Park, which is on the trail.

By road

Take the M60 to jct 16 and then the A666 towards Bolton. Follow the brown signs towards Clifton Country Park.
   OR

By train

The East Lancashire Railway steam train runs from Bury to Summerseat, Ramsbottom, Irwell Vale and Rawtenstall. Contact them (see details on p.49) for timetable and fares.

Overview

The Irwell Sculpture Trail has been (unintentionally) kept a very close secret. It was originally developed in 1993 by three councils (Salford, Rossendale and Bury) in collaboration, to create a 30-mile-long walk with sculptures of public art along the way. The works were either already existing, or have been subsequently commissioned. The sculpture trail follows the old Irwell Valley Way, which was originally just a walkers' route. The whole trail runs from Salford Quays outside Manchester all the way up to Bacup. Wherever possible, it follows the most attractive route, running alongside the River Irwell, the Manchester, Bolton & Bury Canal, through country parks or along the edges of fields.

Works are publicly funded through local grants, but the scheme also won an arts lottery award in 1996. The first sculpture was installed in 1987, and became the first artwork when the trail was started six years later. The trail now has approximately 40 sculptures lining the route (inevitably, some of these are now rather dated and crumbling, though more have been added recently). The idea began as a scheme to help regenerate and improve the use of public areas, but this original proposal has now grown into something more expansive, so it seems a shame that there aren't more people enjoying it. However, there are now plans (for 2010) to build a large art gallery and shopping centre in Radcliffe, which will include some of German artist Ulrich Rückriem's tall standing stones outside, creating a series of columns. It is hoped that this will make people aware of the sculpture trail as a whole by offering a focal point.

Finding your way around

Since the whole trail is too long to cover in detail, I have focused on the most interesting stretch (just under half, approximately 12 miles) which at present has the greatest number of sculptures. Essentially, it covers Radcliffe, Bury and Ramsbottom. If it is longer than you want to walk, you can also walk part (or parts) of it, and drive or take the steam train between different sections (see contact details on p.49).

The trail has remained underused because it has not been well documented in recent years. The last art map was done in 2000 and is now out of print, though a new one is due to be made, which will include all the new work. Photocopied sets of the original 12-page leaflet are given out by the tourist offices in the area (see contact details on

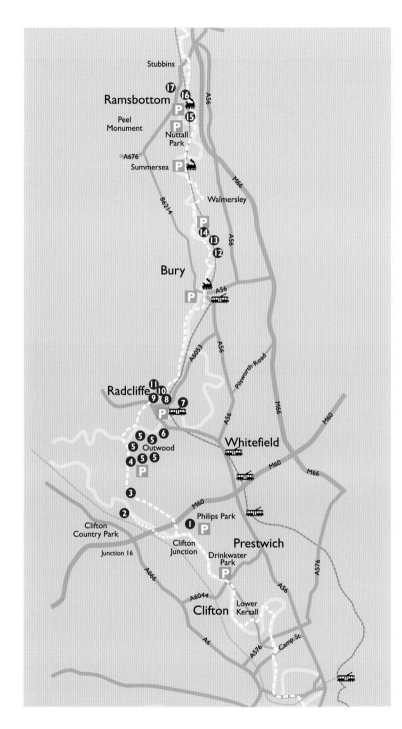

p.48). Usefully, these give very clear written instructions about the route, though unfortunately the maps on them (being photocopies) are at times almost unreadable, and many of the recent artworks are not included. However, combining the written instructions with the art map provides a workable solution. Alternatively, use the new Ordnance Survey (OS) maps showing the Irwell Sculpture Trail, or the old OS maps showing the original Irwell Valley Way. You still need to combine it with the art map, as there are no signposts and sometimes the sculptures are slightly hidden, off the path amongst trees, and thus easily missed. The map shown here includes all the latest pieces on this stretch of the walk. The Irwell Trail website also breaks down the trail into sections, so you can click on each part of the route to see what is there (though unfortunately there are no downloadable maps). It seemed to be slightly tricky to find the start of the trail from wherever you picked it up (though locals were helpful), but once on it the instructions were easy to follow.

If you have the time, you can also include *Dig* in Clifton Country Park – by car this is off the A666, from junction 16 of the M60, or you can walk there, although it does represent a short detour from the main trail.

Irwell Sculpture Trail

1 *Our Seats Are Almost Touching* by Paul Bradley (Philips Park)
2 *Dig* by Rosie Leventon (Clifton Country Park)
3 *Trinity* by Stefan Gec (Outwood Trail)
4 *Northern Mirror* by Alan Johnstone (Outwood, Radcliffe)
5 Untitled works by Ulrich Rückriem (Outwood, Radcliffe)
6 *3* by Mark Jalland (Close Park)
7 *Aeon* by Brass Art (Radcliffe tram station)
8 *Water Made It We*t by Lawrence Weiner (Radcliffe)
9 *Outwood Viaduct* by Janet Lubinska (Radcliffe)
10 *Nailing Home* by Jack Wright (Syrna St, Radcliffe)
11 *In the Bulrushes* by William Pym (at Britannia Mills on Wolsey St)
12 *Waterwheel* by David Kemp (Burrs Country Park)
13 *Picnic Area* by David Fryer (Burrs Country Park)
14 *Stone Cycle* by Julie Edwards (Burrs Country Park)
15 *Seek and You Will Find* by Kerry Morrison (Nuttall Park)
16 *The River* by Hetty Chapman and Karen Allerton (Wharf picnic site, Bridge St)
17 *Tilted Vase* by Edward Allington (Market Place)

Map by Brian Southern, with permission of Bury Council.

The North-west

Things to see

Radcliffe currently has the most recent installation, *Northern Mirror*, located by the road. Viewed straight on, it seems to offer the viewer their own reflection surrounded by industrial cages in an industrial area.

In Burrs Country Park is *Picnic Area*, a giant version of a mouse trap, but this one is designed to catch tourists. This area is a lovely spot – you'll see an old mill with water courses and old mill cottages now used as a café/information centre. *Stone Cycle* is also here.

Ulrich Rückriem has created several sets of standing stones along the path by the former Outwood Colliery, which runs from Radcliffe over the river and on towards Bury. On this very flat and wide route (an old railway path) is a monumental rectangular granite stone standing in the path, and just before it on the right is a small path that leads you to the other standing stones. There are now four pieces by the same artist along this stretch.

above left: *Dig*, by Rosie Leventon, 1999. Haslingden flatrock. Installed at Clifton Country Park. Based on the boats that ferried materials from the wet-earth colliery at Clifton to Salford Quays. *Photo by Alison Stace.*
below left: *Waterwheel*, by David Kemp, 1996. Painted steel and stone. Located in Burrs Country Park. *Photo by Alison Stace.*
opposite: *Enclosure* by Robbie Coleman, 2007. A 100ft diameter neon circle in woods near Orton, at Fred Festival. *Photo ©Tony West, courtesy of Fold.*

9 Fred Festival/Art Invasion

Information:

Tel: 01508 528525
www.fredsblog.com

Location: Sites all across Cumbria
Open: For two weeks in Sept–Oct, check
website for details.
Admission: Free

Overview

This festival of site-specific outdoor installations and artworks takes place at a variety of locations across Cumbria for two weeks in Sept/Oct annually. The festival is put on by the non-profit-making arts organisation Fold, with the aim of bringing contemporary art to a rural environment through a plethora of art installations. The project has been running since 2004 and includes a range of international artists as well as local talent. The work changes every year and projects vary massively; the pieces in 2007 included a ring of reflected light from the estuary mud by Paul Clark, and *Shake Pole* by Richard Box, consisting of 80 metres of small fluorescent tubes installed under electricity pylons, which would glow with changing colours when approached and go out when touched. *Romantic Seduction and Power,* by Mark Haywood and Amanda Newall, included a field of toy windmills; Morecambe Bay beach was scattered with ceramic knickers by Helen Fletcher; a giant wild boar was constructed from fleece by Jan Hicks; a giant bubble was created by Steve Messam over a redundant building; and Avril Douglas made strange creatures from found materials to line a 3-mile stretch of the Pennine Way.

This fantastic variety of installations is worth visiting, with the only problems being that they are not all up for the whole duration of the festival (some are only on for a couple of days – obviously works and locations change each year, so check website), and for visitors from further afield, the large area that the works cover makes it hard to see all of them without travelling around a great deal. It is worth looking closely at the website for details on each work for ones that interest you. The festival does bring in a great influx of people to the area, so if booking trains and B&Bs, get organised early to keep costs down. This really needs a car to get around, or alternatively a lot of time and careful planning.

The Midlands

- Gloucestershire • Herefordshire • Worcestershire
- Warwickshire • Shropshire • Staffordshire • West Midlands
- Derbyshire • Leicestershire • Northamptonshire
- Lincolnshire • Nottinghamshire

10 Jerwood Sculpture Park at Ragley Hall

11 Forest of Dean Sculpture Trail

12 Ironbridge Open-air Museum

13 Meadow Gallery (not on map)

14 Burghley House

Other Places of Interest

15 Newnham Paddox Art Park

16 Coventry Canal Art Trail

17 Quenington Sculpture Trust

18 Chatsworth House & Garden

10 Jerwood Sculpture Park at Ragley Hall

Oracle, by Michael Ayrton, 1963–4. Bronze.
Photo by Dave Morgan, courtesy of Jerwood Sculpture Park.

Information:

Ragley Hall, Alcester, Warwickshire, B49 5NJ.
Tel: 0800 093 0290 / 020 7388 6287
www.jerwoodsculpture.org

Facilities: Café, toilets, gift shop, adventure playground, lake and sailing club
Open: (summer 2007) 22 Mar–30 Sep, Thu–Sun only (plus Bank Holidays) 10am–6pm; open daily in spring and summer school holidays.
Admission: £8.50 adults, £5 children, £7 senior citizens, £27 families (2 adults, 3 kids)
Time needed: 2–2½ hours

Getting there

By road
From the south, take the A46 to Alcester, then follow brown signs to Ragley Hall.
From the north, take the A435 to Alcester. Just before Alcester, at large roundabout with lots of brown signs, take 2nd exit (signposted Ragley Hall). • After the village of Arrow the entrance is on your right.

By train
Stratford-upon-Avon train station, then 15 minutes by taxi, or Evesham station then 15 minutes by taxi.

Overview

Jerwood Sculpture Park has some of the best sculpture set in spectacular grounds. There are lots of other amenities at Ragley Hall, including the beautiful grounds, landscaped by Capability Brown, and a café in a marquee overlooking the lake. Ragley Hall was already an attraction before the Jerwood Foundation moved its sculpture collection here in 2004. So the sculpture park was an afterthought, and just occasionally you feel that pieces have been tucked out of the way so as not to ruin the view. The sculpture collection takes a leisurely 2½ hours to see, and is made up of three different parts: classic modern British sculpture; works from the biennial Jerwood Sculpture Prize; and other independent pieces commissioned by the Foundation. Overall, the sculpture is mainly by modern British artists, and most of the work in the park is permanent. Although there are not a great number of pieces (17 at the time of visiting), the sculpture is of very high quality – having been through a rigorous selection process – and all by very well-established sculptors. The Jerwood Sculpture Prize has been running since 2001, and there are currently three sculptures by prize-winners in the grounds – the fourth is due to be installed some time in 2008. Amongst the works on display are pieces by Antony Gormley, Kenneth Armitage, Peter Hayes and Elisabeth Frink; most have been cast in bronze. Incidentally, the life-size sculptures of children running and playing by the pond are not part of the collection. Well worth a visit.

Finding your way around

Go up the long drive through the estate grounds until you reach a wooden kiosk. Here when you pay make sure you ask for the Jerwood Foundation map of the sculptures in the park and the list of artists with information on each piece. The black and white sheet has the sculptures in both the garden and the woodland walk. This map can also be downloaded from the internet. There is parking in several places on the estate, but if you take the right-hand fork of the road after the kiosk (signposted for Jerwood Sculpture), this will bring you to the stables, where the trail starts.

It is best if you follow the numbered sequence on the map, as the trail takes you around the edge of the gardens and is fairly clear – pieces are positioned to give you a good view as you round a corner. If you do the reverse sequence in the garden, make sure you look out for the work, as from this direction some pieces are tucked away quite discreetly behind hedges and could be missed. Benedict Carpenter's *Universal Object* actually lies just outside the far garden gate.

Once you have seen everything in the garden, which takes about 1½ hours to go round, you will need to retrace your steps towards Alan Thornhill's *Bond* and Lynn Chadwick's *Cloaked Figure* (currently numbers 3 and 2), as the path to the woodland walk is located nearby. Follow the signposts out of the garden and across the field. You

will see the gate at the other end. The woodland walk is approximately 1½ miles long and takes about 30 minutes, but allow some time to admire the view from the top of the hill. After you've seen the *Standing Stone* by Sara More, the signposts will direct you off the main path onto a path on your left, taking you up a small hill. Walk towards the benches ahead of you and as you emerge from the trees you will find an amazing view looking towards the house.

The landscape has been beautifully thought out, with a line of trees directing your gaze towards the house, so make sure you do not miss the *Oracle*, tucked into the line of trees on your left as you descend.

opposite: *Cloaked Figure IX,* by Lynn Chadwick, 1978. Bronze.
above: *Insider VIII,* by Antony Gormley, 1998. Iron. *Photos by Dave Morgan, courtesy of Jerwood Sculpture Park.*

Things to see

All the work here is of a very high standard. Within the gardens I found Lynn Chadwick's *Cloaked Figure*, standing amongst the trees, a very regal and dominating figure. Its abstract head means that there are no features to read, adding to its mystery and solitude. The sharp angular head is echoed in the sharp angle of the cloak behind it. It is a very self-contained figure, appearing not to need other people, and thus it is perfectly situated on a slight hill so that the viewer is forced to look up to it slightly, reinforcing its superiority.

As you walk round a bend in the path you will find *The Crusader*, by Harry Everington, on a small area of grass, charging off towards the edge of the gardens and the open parkland. This piece was one of my favourites. It has so much movement, energy and decisiveness. Indeed, although stone was his first love, Everington modelled this piece first in clay in order to work at a faster speed and get across the emotions seen on the faces of horse and rider. All the lines in his body are defined in a forward movement, and his horse seems part of that same dynamic gesture.

Insider VIII, by Antony Gormley, is so thin that I almost passed it by. The piece is one of his earlier works (1998), and thus not in the recognisable body-cast shapes that he is now known for, so it is interesting to see how his work has evolved. The aim of this piece was to reduce his body to one third of its original mass. He wanted to reduce not just the physical presence but also the subconscious mass, so that what you are left with is the essence of the man, the person inside the mass.

Just outside the gates at the end of the garden's sculpture trail, you will find *Universal Object* by Benedict Carpenter, which won the first Jerwood Sculpture Prize in 2001. It lies very close to the cattle grid, which struck me as an odd place to site it. The intention behind this strange-looking but fascinating object is that it will be recognised by everyone as something – though what specifically is less certain. The object functions in the same way as the Rorschach test, the famous

left: *Widow Woman* by Ronald Rae, 1992. Granite.
right: *The Crusader* by Harry Everington, 1992. Bronze. *Photos by Dave Morgan, courtesy of Jerwood Sculpture Park.*

ink-blot test that suggests shapes to the viewer, and is used by psychologists to see what is in a patient's mind. In a similar way each individual will see the beginnings of many different shapes in this piece as they try to make sense of it.

Descending through the avenue of trees towards the house, you will see Michael Ayrton's *Oracle* tucked in amongst them. This strange-looking piece has a real pres-ence about it. The apparently thoughtful pose of this hybrid of human and alien elements seems to emanate power and knowledge. Not surprisingly, it appears that the artist was greatly influenced by Greek sculpture. This large, silent figure could surely tell us all we needed to know, if only we had the power to understand. It could do with a slightly more prominent position.

Finally, down by the lakeside you will find Ronald Rae's *Widow Woman*. The piece looks like it has been carved from an old boulder that just happened to be there, though this is obviously not the case. However, it seems that Rae is a sculptor who works with the intrinsic properties of each stone, letting its natural flow and curve suggest the form that emerges. This very emotional piece, carved out of granite, seems to sit perfectly in the landscape, conveying waves of sadness out across the water.

11 Forest of Dean Sculpture Trail

Information:

Beechenhurst Lodge,
Speech House Rd, Broadwell, Coleford,
Gloucestershire, GL16 7EG
Tel: 01594 827357
www.forestofdean-sculpture.org.uk

Facilities: Toilets, café serving hot and cold
drinks, sandwiches and hot meals, and sell-
ing maps of the sculpture trail.
Open: Daily, Apr–Oct, 10am–6pm,
Nov–Mar, 10am–5pm
Admission: Free (car park £3)
Time needed: 3 hours

right: *House* by Miles Davies, 1988. Steel. *Photo
by Alison Stace, by permission of the Forest of
Dean Trust.*
far right: *Cathedral* by Kevin Atherton, 1986.
*Photo by Alison Stace, by permission of the
Forest of Dean Trust.*

Getting there

By road

From the south, take the M4 towards Wales as far as jct 20, then the M48 towards Chepstow. Cross the Severn Bridge (toll is approx. £5). Over the bridge turn left at the junction towards Chepstow (A466). • At the roundabout on the edge of Chepstow turn right onto the A48 towards Gloucester. Drive through Chepstow and once over the bridge take the next sharp left turn towards Coleford (up the steep hill into Tutshill). • At the mini-roundabout turn right towards Coleford on the B4228. • In Coleford you come to a crossroads with traffic lights and the King's Head Hotel, turn right here (signposted Cinderford, Speech House, Gloucester). About 300 yards along turn right again (signposted Cinderford, Speech House) onto Bakers Hill. • Go up the hill and down again – pass the recycle centre and Hopewell Colliery on your left. Go straight over the crossroads at the bottom and as it climbs again take left turn signposted Sculpture Trail and Beechenhurst Lodge.

From the north, take the M5 south, and at Jct 11a take the A417 to Gloucester, then follow the A40 to the A48. • Follow A48 and take right turn signposted Cinderford (with petrol station at corner). • Go up hill to Littledean, and right at mini-roundabout. • Continue out of Littledean up the hill and take left turn on middle of the bend (signposted Speech House and Coleford) onto the B4226. • Follow this road through residential area and on towards Coleford. Pass Dikes Hospital on your right, and further on Speech House Hotel on your left. The road dips down with a bend and Beechenhurst Lodge entrance is on the right side just after the big bend.

By train:

Lydney Station, and 15 minutes by taxi.

Overview

The Forest of Dean Sculpture Trail is one of the oldest outdoor sculpture venues. A great combination of trees and art, this trail is a manageable length, although there is a fair walk between sculptures. The Forest of Dean itself is an ancient royal forest with a long history. Still a working forest, it has also been designated a National Forest Nature Reserve, meaning that some areas and trees are protected. First opened in 1986, the trail was originally initiated by Martin Orrom (from the Forestry Commission) in partnership with Rupert Martin and Jeremy Rees (from the Arnolfini Gallery in Bristol). The main idea was to allow artists to express their interpretation of the forest and its history, rather than for the forest to be a beautiful gallery for pre-designed pieces. All the invited artists first come to the forest to choose a site for their work, before planning their sculpture. The work is therefore very much site-specific, a response from the artist to the forest, the hope being that the sculpture will encourage the public to venture further into the woods and to think about the forest itself. This is different from Grizedale Forest, where work is often conceived beforehand and then placed in suitable locations. Setting up a sculpture trail has also changed the character of the Forest of Dean, as it involved setting up proper paths with signposts in order to help people to find the work. Carolyn Black, who works for the Sculpture Trust, feels it is important to remind people that, despite the new emphasis on destinations that the signposts obviously bring, the journey between the works – the experience of the forest itself – is as important as the sculptures.

Naturally, the forest changes massively from season to season, and sculptures can look completely different amongst bluebells or autumn leaves or bare windswept trees. The trail being one of the oldest, some of the original works that have fallen apart or become too dangerous to leave have recently been removed or replaced. For instance, Sophie Ryder's herd of deer has been replaced with a single stag in a different location, while Ian Hamilton Finlay's stone *Grove of Silence* and *Melissa's Swing* by Peter Appleton have recently been repaired.

The Forestry Commission and the Sculpture Trust work as a partnership, the Sculpture Trust overseeing the planning and commissioning of works, and the Forestry Commission maintaining them. Most of the sculptures here are permanent works, though the Trust has held some innovative temporary events over the years including *Light Shift* (2001) and *Reveal* (2006) two night-time exhibitions using light and sound. On a more regular basis, however, smaller events are held, and guided walks have recently been introduced, often led by a featured artist or another guest speaker, in which a variety of subjects relating to the sculpture and the forest are discussed – check the website for updates on these.

Finding your way around

The café sells maps of the sculpture trail, and although the way is clearly marked, without a map you may miss a few sculptures as they are sometimes off the path and not immediately noticeable amongst all the trees. There are currently 18 sculptures spaced out on a circular walk – although a new work by Annie Cattrell was due to be installed in early 2008. The trail starts in front of Beechenhurst Lodge (which houses the café and toilets) and is clearly marked with a large post. The map currently sends people around the trail in one direction, starting with the enormous chair (*Place*) that can be seen away in front of you as you head up the path from the Lodge. All the paths for the sculpture trail are clearly marked with posts – the tops of these are painted blue, with arrows on the sides indicating which direction to go in. Make sure you follow only the blue posts for the sculpture trail, as other posts with different colours are markers for other walks! The only path where this system seemed to fail was at a junction after *Hanging Fire*, where suddenly some new paths appear, leading off to the right – do not take these paths as they lead back into the forest (there is a somewhat hidden marker pointing the right way). The whole walk takes about three hours (as always this depends on your speed, stamina and the time spent looking at each work) but you can cut off about 20 minutes at the end if you wish by backtracking slightly after *Melissa's Swing* and then turning right at the corner to take a short cut back to the Lodge.

An alternative to the usual route is to go round backwards. Having seen the first piece, entitled *Place* (resembling a giant's chair), you could turn right towards what is currently the final work, *Melissa's Swing*, and continue round that way. The reason for doing this is to approach *Cathedral* (a suspended stained-glass window), as well as a couple of sculptures further on, along the vast long path through the trees, and thus get the best experience of it. Currently you come across it sideways, and the drama is somehow diminished. The map is due to be redone, so the route may change, but remember that in order to go round backwards, you need to follow the arrows in reverse! The paths are clearly marked, so providing you have the map this should not be too difficult.

far left: *Iron Road,* by Keir Smith, 1986. Jarrah wood sleepers. *Photo by Alison Stace, by permission of the Forest of Dean Trust.*
left: *Hanging Fire,* by Cornelia Parker, 1986. *Photo by Alison Stace, by permission of the Forest of Dean Trust.*

The Midlands

Things to see

The 18 sculptures currently featured are all permanent, and some have been there since the trail first opened. Gradually over the years, a few sculptures have disintegrated and a few more have arrived. Some were originally made from bracken and twigs and were never intended to survive. Some, however, are now over two decades old. Magdalena Jetelova's *Place*, for instance, was installed in 1986. This has become the sculpture trail's iconic piece, and the one that everyone remembers and recognises. Its monumental structure seems a fantastic viewpoint from which to survey the landscape. Standing next to it makes you feel you have been transported to Lilliput, that humankind is no longer the dominant species, and that whoever owns the chair, has just gone off to roam the woods and could return at any time. The chair's huge proportions and rough tree trunks make it appear perfectly at home, even in charge, in the forest. Suddenly, it is human beings that don't belong here.

Dead Wood – Bois Mort, by Carole Drake, represents tombs in the forest – great slabs of stone hidden in the woods, some of which are marked and some not, reminding us of the unmarked graves of dead soldiers perhaps, and the use of forests as burial grounds, provoking the idea of forests as keepers of secrets and memories. The plaques on some of the stones have images etched into them of the French forests devastated during the Great War – perhaps a memorial to all the dead woods, wherever they may be.

Fire and Water Boats, also by David Nash, is another of the trail's original sculptures, and is perfectly situated by a manmade watercourse. Primitive canoe shapes situated in a watery bog next to the stream, they return us to some of the essentials of man and the elements – fire, water, wood, transport, fishing. Simultaneously, they also refer to the history of the forest: the charred wood, while in one respect an aesthetic decision, is also a reference to charcoal manufacture, while the canoes evoke the boats that carried the coal once mined in this area.

Keir Smith created *Iron Road* by laying 20 carved wood sleepers to replicate a railway on the site of what was once a railway line that ran through the forest; if you look in both directions you can see the perfectly flat gentle curve that it followed. As the sleepers are laid out on what is now the path, you are forced to engage with the forest's past – in fact you are walking along it; this sculpture simply focuses your attention on that fact. As you walk alongside the sleepers, you notice that each one has a different carving in its centre. These refer to the history of the forest, though some are clearer than others. At the end (second to last) the face of the artist is depicted as the wind, or perhaps just among the clouds. The symbols and the overall narrative are open to interpretation.

The tall and skinny form of *House*, by Miles Davies, rises up into the canopy of the trees, forcing you to look up at the tops of the trees surrounding you. My favourite piece here, it engages the viewer on many levels. Its form replicates a forest mineshaft; normally a structure above ground with a roof providing cover, with the shaft going deep into the ground, in this case the whole structure has been brought above ground, so that

above: *Place* by Magdalena Jetelova, 1986. *Photo by Carolyn Black, courtesy of the Forest of Dean Trust.*
right: *Fire and Water Boats* by David Nash, 1986. *Photo by Alison Stace, by permission of the Forest of Dean Trust.*

The Midlands

the little house is among the tree tops. The security and safety of the house has become the shelter offered by the forest. The tall, straight legs replicate the shape of the neighbouring trees so that it fits in perfectly with its surroundings – despite it also being a house removed from its usual context. An austerity and a stillness also seem to surround it, while its architectural qualities stand out well against the trees. A work of many perspectives making us view the world in a new way – quite literally!

Bruce Allan's *Observatory*, from 1988, can be found next to the Cannop Ponds. This somewhat surreal staircase at first seems to lead nowhere, but is actually offering a viewpoint in the tree canopy from which to look down on the woods and water – again altering our perspective. It is a place simply to stop and absorb the surroundings. The forest has become the work we are to contemplate, while the piece itself is not so much a work to be seen – its form is not that important – but one to be used and experienced.

A more recent addition to the collection (2001), Neville Gabie's *Raw* is a giant cube made from a felled oak (one of the Navy oaks planted in the 1800s) cut into squared pieces and put together like a giant puzzle in order to make up the cube. As much of the wood as possible was used. The whole piece is held together in the old fashioned way by using wooden pegs, and the stump of the felled tree can be seen next to it. Neville Gabie had become fascinated by the life and volume of a tree – how much water does it consume? How much wood does it contain? How do you measure the volume of such an irregular shape? *Raw* is the tree reduced to its essential element – wood. The cube itself has a fantastic pattern of squares and gives a lovely glow in the summer light. However, one could question whether it is right to cut down a 200-year-old oak in order to make art that draws the viewer's attention to the ancient forest and its trees.

12 Ironbridge Open-air Museum of Steel Sculpture

Information:

Moss House, Cherry Tree Hill, Coalbrookdale,
Telford, Shropshire, TF8 7EF.
Tel: 01952 433152
www.go2.co.uk/steelsculpture

Facilities: Toilets, educational workshops
throughout the year. (NB: there is nowhere
on site to buy food or drink, so remember to
eat first, or bring a picnic with you – as long
as you take away your litter.)
Open: 1 March–30 November, Tue–Sun,
10am–5pm. Open Bank Holiday Mondays.
Summer evening visits by advance booking.
Admission: £3 (£2.50 each for groups of ten
or more), £2 for concessions (£1.50 each for
groups of ten or more), and £8 for a family
of up to two adults & three children.
Time needed: 2–3 hours.

far right: *Inclined Impasse,* by Roy Kitchin, 1982.
Photo by Coral Lambert.
right: A Flower in Flower, by Keir Smith, 2001.
*Photo by Pam Brown, both courtesy of Ironbridge
Open Air Museum.*

Getting there

By road

Exit the M54 at jct 4 onto the A442, then turn off the A442 onto the A4169 shortly afterwards. • At the next roundabout go straight over, following signs for the A4169. Ignore the signs directing you left to Ironbridge Museums, but instead follow signs to the Museum of Steel Sculpture. • Pass Lightmoor Rd on your right, and Brick Kiln Bank on your left (somewhat hidden by bushes), then take the next left onto Cherry Tree Hill (the museum is signposted). Ignore the first turning on your left. • You will see the Ironbridge Museum on your right further down with a large sculpture next to it. Park here or in the overspill car park further down to your left, open during busy seasons.

By train

Telford Central station then taxi (approx. 7 mins).

Overview

If you like your sculptures larger than life and made of metal, then this museum is certainly the place for you. Set up by Pam Brown and Roy Kitchin, two sculpture artists, the project was from the beginning a labour of love. Sadly, Roy died in 1997 (he is buried beside his sculpture *Blake* in the grounds). Pam now has the task of single-handedly running and maintaining the grounds, as well as organising the summer workshops, but everything runs remarkably efficiently. Today the museum operates as both a sculpture park and a centre for education and creativity.

A long time in the planning, the open-air museum was originally set up as a site on which Roy and Pam could display their work, instead of constantly moving work around for temporary exhibitions, which was both costly and time-consuming. Roy felt that generally pieces

were moved on from a site 'before the landscape had a chance to understand and accept them'. In 1980 they began looking for some unused land, and their cry was answered by the Telford Development Corporation. The site finally agreed upon in 1984 had originally been the Cherry Tree Hill brick and tile works, and needed large amounts of clearance and landscaping, much of which was done by hand with wheelbarrows. The museum gradually grew into a much larger project, and other artists were invited to include their work on site.

The museum's site in Coalbrookdale was chosen because of its proximity to the most recognisable structure in the area where the iron industry really took off, Abraham Darby III's Iron Bridge spanning the River Severn, built in 1779. The museum grounds stand on a ten-acre site with wild woodland and open grass areas, hidden enclosures and deep tree-filled gullies. A large number of sculptures (74 at the last count) are scattered throughout the park; it is a strange experience to be surrounded by so much sculpture in one medium. The largest and heaviest of these (the biggest weighs in at four tons) can be found on the open grass of the top field. Most of the sculptures here are huge, and many are either on permanent exhibition or long-term loan from the artists. There are also plans to hold some short-term exhibitions.

The museum and house have been built in the style of a factory from the time of the Industrial Revolution (NB: apart from the toilets, access to this building is only for those taking part in workshops). The museum holds many maquettes of the work on display outside, and combines workshop areas (such as the woodwork area upstairs) with a study and bedroom. Downstairs is the enormous steel workshop, which has double doors to allow for the movement of work, as many pieces and parts are built on site.

The workshop also houses the equipment used for the steel workshops in the summer. These are the only educational steel courses in the country, and therefore always oversubscribed – so ring for details and book early if you're interested! A group of Americans made up of students and practising artists come over every summer to 'crew' the foundry. The sculpture in the grounds also functions as the focus of poetry workshops held at the museum, and are run by a professional creative writer over long weekends.

above: *Blake,* by Roy Kitchin, 1982. *Photo by unknown photographer courtesy of Ironbridge Open Air Museum.*
right: *E.X.P.,* by Roy Kitchin, 1982. *Photo by Coral Lambert, courtesy of Ironbridge Open Air Museum.*

The Midlands

Finding your way around

The reception to the sculpture park is at one of the building's front windows. Tap on the window for attention, but if nobody is in, you are welcome to look around the grounds anyway; you'll find a wooden honesty/donations box for your payment and another with maps of the park. These boxes (located in front of and to the right-hand side of the house just off the car park) stand next to the small path leading into the woods, which is the entrance to the grounds. In fact, it doesn't hugely matter where you start as, although the gravel paths are marked on the map, there is no set route to follow. Do not try to follow the numbers of the sculptures in order, as you will see they are not sequential! The numbers you can see on the cast-iron plaques do correspond, however, to the list of sculptures on the back, and are also identified on the map, so you can use them to navigate by if your map-reading is up to scratch. Otherwise, this is really a place just to wander around and see what catches your eye, or as Pam says, 'here you can be completely free'! This does mean you may miss work unless you concentrate, so be sure to see the top field which runs alongside the A4169, and is marked as the long open area in the top-left half of the map. This is where some of the most impressive sculptures can be found, although there are interesting pieces tucked away all over the place.

It took us several hours of wandering around to see every piece, though this involved walking slowly and discussing each one. If you want to see everything, allow time for meandering back and forth.

Things to see

If you decide to head off into the woods at the start of the path by the post boxes, one of the first pieces you will find is *Roata* (50), up to your right. Look closely at this twisting and turning piece, and you will realise it is actually figurative; the head can be seen sticking out near the bottom. It was made by Katherine Gili, who hired a contortionist to pose for her while she drew her designs.

Mechanical Arch (12), by Roy Kitchin, is one of the larger sculptures in the park and entirely dominates its display area, even while surrounded by tall trees on three sides; you can almost see its chest puff out as you approach. Strangely, the thing that made this sculpture for me was the wonderful 'look at me' colour, a striking rusty orange-brown, which perfectly complements the surrounding greenery.

Up on the top field several of the large pieces are worth noting. In the far right-hand corner is *Amphitrite* (14) by Michael Lyons, a funky arrangement of flat blue pieces of steel. Lyons always begins the design process using cut-out pieces of black card on white paper, and indeed this piece looks very different from front and back: if you go to the far side of it, by the hedge, you can see the fabulous silhouetted shape, and envisage how it must have looked at the concept stage. It is also, at four tons, the heaviest work in the museum's collection.

Tucked into a corner along the left-hand stretch is *Surveyor* (16) by Pam Brown. This

enormous version of a viewfinder gives great vistas of greenery and the land beyond, framed and shaped by the intersection of the circle and the V. As you walk around it, this intersection and framed view shifts constantly, offering a great backdrop to these simple shapes, which seem to create their own, changing composition. The piece does have echoes of a giant gun support, and Pam herself said that when it was installed a military helicopter flew over from the local base, came back, and lowered right down to check that it wasn't some giant piece of terrorist machinery.

In the middle of the left-hand side is the amazing *Swing Bridge* (71), the only kinetic piece of sculpture at the museum. The piece is purely wind-powered, and its perfect balance means the very steady, slow, even swing suggested by the title needs only a very slight breeze to work. The lovely cast wave-like forms at both ends of the piece just

completed it for me. The artist, Gerry Masse, comes every summer to help with the workshops and is now setting up his own Sculpture Trails outdoor museum in Indiana (www.sculpturetrails.com).

On the lower part of the grounds in a circular area of its own stands *A Flower in Flower* (67), a wonderfully peaceful sculpture that glimmers as it catches the light. It was made by Keir Smith, upon discovering he had leukaemia, as a sort of monument to Roy Kitchin, who died of the disease. Sadly, Keir Smith also died recently. As you look up, it seems entwined with the ivy and oak behind it.

above: *Amphitrite,* by Michael Lyons, 1993. *Photo by Alison Stace.*
right: *Swan,* by Daphne Wright. Cast marble, Meadow Gallery commission, 2007. *Photo courtesy of the Meadow Gallery.*

13 Meadow Gallery

Information:

Office only: Meadow Gallery, Cumberley, Cumberley Lane, Hope Bagot, Ludlow, SY8 3LJ.
Tel: 01584 891659
www.meadowgallery.co.uk

Facilities: Each exhibition is usually located in the grounds of a large stately home or similar, so generally there are toilets and a café on site.
Open: Depends on the venue, so ring or check the website for details.
Admission: Depends on venue, so once again check for details.

Getting there

The location changes for every exhibition, so ring or check the website for details.

The Midlands

Overview

Before you go rushing out the door to visit, stop! This gallery is actually an organisation that puts on exhibitions of contemporary sculpture in a different location every year. Normally housed in the grounds of large stately homes, and always located in the Midlands – these exhibitions are usually on for three or four months every year over the summer. The organisation operates as a sort of mobile gallery, trying to present sculpture in an outdoor context while at the same time offering an alternative to sculpture trails and permanent installations. The gallery aims to encourage existing and established artists to try making work for an outdoor setting, which may be a new experience for them.

The last few exhibitions were Still Life, at Hanbury Hall, Worcestershire (2007), Vertigo, at Sudeley Castle, Gloucestershire (2005), and Mappa Mundi, at Burford House, near Ludlow, Shropshire (2004). Mappa Mundi featured sculpture by Stephen Cox, who made *Granite Catamarans on a Granite Wave*, at Goodwood (see p. 100).

Things to see

The work changes with every exhibition, but is always of a high standard and generally features well-known artists. Past exhibitions have included work by Stephen Cox, Damien Hirst, Daphne Wright, Paul Morrison, Franz West and Mariele Neudecker amongst many others. Check their website for a full list of past exhibitions, artists and work.

Souvenir of England by Jane Prophet, Meadow Gallery Commission, 2007. *Photo courtesy of the Meadow Gallery.*

14 Burghley Sculpture Garden

Information:

Burghley House, Stamford, Lincolnshire,
PE9 3JY.
Tel: 01780 752451
www.burghley.co.uk

Facilities: Toilets, café (in summer), educational programmes, brewhouse (visitors centre), 'Gardens of Surprise'
Open: (garden) all year 11am–5pm: (house) not open Fridays, otherwise 25 March–30 Oct, 11am–4.30pm.
Admission: (adults) £6.60 for gardens, (children) £3.30 (free from Nov–March).
Time needed: 1 ½ hours.

Seeds of Time, by Stephen Beardsell. Hot blown glass. From the temporary exhibition, 2007. *Photo courtesy of Burghley Sculpture Garden.*

Getting there

By road

• From the north take A1 south. After passing Grantham turn left onto A43 towards Stamford. From the south take the A1 heading north, continue along as it becomes the A1(M) past jct 17, and then after you pass the junction with the A47, you will come to a roundabout (with Stamford marked straight ahead). Turn right onto the B1081 and continue past stone gates on your right. • You will come into a pretty village (Stamford) full of old stone-built houses, and see a pub called the Bull & Swan. Turn into the small road that runs down the left-hand side of this pub. • Continue along this road until you see a blue sign saying 'Visitors' Entrance'. From the car park, two curved halves of a tree trunk with 'sculpture garden' written along them will guide you to the sculpture entrance.

By train

Nearest large station is Peterborough, then 20 mins by taxi. Or change at Peterborough by train to Stamford station and walk through park (30 mins) or 5 mins by taxi.

right: *Balance*, by Sophie Dickens. *Photo courtesy of Burghley Sculpture Garden.*
far right: *Pure Pollen*, (water piece) by Matthew Lane Sanderson. *Photo courtesy of Burghley Sculpture Garden.*

The Midlands

Overview

Burghley House is a stately home with beautiful gardens and a lake. The sculpture gardens have been reclaimed from Capability Brown's lost lower gardens, with work carefully scattered throughout to make the most of all areas.

Pick up the leaflet with the map of the gardens, as more work is added every year – often after the summer exhibitions. The sculptures marked on the map are all permanent (about 18 pieces), but every year from April to October there is also an exhibition in the gardens of work for sale. Some of these pieces have subsequently been donated as permanent fixtures. Some of the work is of a very high standard while some is not so impressive, but for half the year this assessment includes exhibition work, which is only temporary and not featured on their maps. Overall, though there are a few great pieces in the permanent collection, hardened sculpture buffs may be a little disappointed. Burghley seems like a sculpture garden that has not yet reached its potential, though it is no doubt still evolving as time goes on. Whatever it lacks, though, it certainly makes up for in wonderful surroundings.

Finding your way around

The maps at the entrance kiosk show a plan of the gardens indicating where the various pieces are sited (temporary exhibitions are not marked on this map). There is no set route, but, broadly speaking, the path takes you alongside the lake and around the gardens in a big circle – although there is also work to be found in the middle. It takes about an hour and a half to see everything – and you do need to wander back and forth a bit to get your bearings and to find certain things – but you could easily stay longer just to enjoy the grounds and the other things on offer.

Things to see

Vertical Face, by Rick Kirby, is a giant face in a lovely rusty colour, made from small pieces of steel attached to a larger framework. The face is not complete: the back is open so that you can see the framework and the edges of the face are not finished – it is almost a rough drawing in 3D, showing enough of the features to give you a broad idea of the whole face, and letting your brain fill in the rest. It has great presence and drama, and currently stands a little way from the edge of a large circular area, which at the time of visiting was marked out by tall black vases, suggesting an arena or an amphitheatre. Viewed from the bench at the other side of this dip (which may be the remains of an old pond), you feel as if the lions and entertainers will arrive at any minute.

Above the path that runs alongside the lake is a huge tree with a large branch stretching overhead, along which three wooden figures appear to balance. The appropriately named *Balance*, by Sophie Dickens, has movement and poise, conveying the exact feeling of someone walking nervously along a narrow branch, precariously balancing above the path. I loved it, but as it is so high up it was hard to see the figures against the light and through the leaves, although this could be

left: *5 Carved Oak Trunks* by Giles Kent. *Photo courtesy of Burghley Sculpture Garden.*
right: *Vertical Face* by Rick Kirby. *Photo courtesy of Burghley Sculpture Garden.*

more or less of a problem depending on the time of day or year. It is also true that the figures need the height to convey the sense of fear. (Sophie Dickens also had a set of wooden cartwheeling figures on the ground at Pride of the Valley Sculpture Park which are currently being cast in bronze.) The *Five Carved Oak Trunks*, by Giles Kent, that span

the lake look better in real life than in images – they really integrate with their location and environment, their simple organic forms reflecting well in the water and echoing the shapes of reeds nearby.

By the path is a large disc of slate suspended in glass, *Untitled*, by Martyn Barratt. The

piece itself I felt was fascinating, but the way it was displayed needed rethinking, or at least perhaps softening with plants to hide the distracting, heavy framework that supports it.

There are always some interesting pieces in the summer exhibitions, and some of these will remain.

Other Places of Interest

15 Newnham Paddox Art Park

Information:

Newnham Paddox House, Newnham Paddox,
Monks Kirby, Warwickshire, CV23ORX
Tel: 01788 833513
www.newnhampaddox.com

Facilities: None
Open: Mid-May–1st week in Oct (exact dates
vary each year, so check website or ring for
details).
Admission: Adults £4, concessions £3, children (age 5-15) £1.
Time needed: 1– 1 ½ hours

Getting there

By road
• Take M1 to jct 18 then take A5 over four
roundabouts. At Magna Park roundabout
leave the A5, following signs to Willey. Look
for signposts 1.8 miles along on the left.
OR
• From M40 take Banbury exit (jct 11)
then A423 to Princethorpe, then B4455
(towards Leicester). • Turn right towards
Willey and Lutterworth and look for signposts from here.

right: *Herne the Hunter* by Michael Rizzello (dcd
2005), exhibited 2004–2007. Bronze. *Photo courtesy of Newnham Paddox Art Park.*
opposite left: *Boris* by Lorne McKean & Edwin
Russell. Bronze resin. Exhibited in 2007.
far right: *Cheetahs,* by Lucy Kinsella. Bronze
resin. Her work can also be seen at Pride of the
Valley. Exhibited in 2007. *Photos by Alison Stace.*

Overview

Newnham Paddox Art Park has been open for five years. Run by the Denbighs (Alex Denbigh is now the 12th Earl of Denbigh), who have given up the city life to return to the Denbigh family's estate, it has the potential to develop into something quite exciting, but is currently still in a process of growth and change. The grounds were originally landscaped by Capability Brown in 1753–7, but the last of the original houses became a drain on the family's resources, and having been altered and butchered over successive generations, it was finally demolished in the 1950s. This enabled the land, woods and farms to be preserved for future generations. The grounds have a beautiful lake containing carp (recently opened for fishing), and there are ancient trees of many varieties.

The park is currently run as a summer gallery, with work changing every year (though some pieces stay on). The work shown is in a variety of media, including wood, steel, marble, ceramic and bronze resin, and by a changing collection of artists. There are on average about 60 works on display (again, this varies from year to year – the biggest show had 130). Several pieces arrive here from Chelsea after the flower show. With two small children, the Denbighs are keen to make the place family-friendly, so they also run family days, with storytellers and workshops for children, and welcome school groups. The plan at the moment is for a gradual change in direction from a gallery-orientated park, with selling shows, to becoming a not-for-profit enterprise, with more permanent installations (there are two already) as well as workshops in collaboration with Education 4 Conservation. During this gradual shift the two aspects will run concurrently.

The temporary sculpture varies quite dramatically in medium, style and quality. There are some lovely pieces and some very modern abstract works (such as *Demeter* by Roger Stephens), as well as animals, figurative pieces and slightly darker, more off-the-wall works.

Things to see

From the animals on display when I visited, *Boris* (the dog) is an almost permanent fixture and a popular sculpture in bronze resin by Lorne McKean, sitting under the trees with a very sad and expressive face. There were also some wonderful *Cheetahs on a Rock* by Tom Joynson, which were both realistic and expressive. On a more abstract level, the *Utopian Horse* in steel was fantastic, made from an old boiler tank, which has been cut up and rearranged, and would be perfectly at home at the Ironbridge Museum (see pp. 66–70).

The best piece of abstract art on show was *Demeter* by Roger Stephens. This tall and elegant figurative piece was reminiscent of a pregnant woman, and stands by the edge of the water looking out across the lake. This simple work has a calm quality that owes something to Moore and Hepworth.

There are two permanent installations currently at the park, and the plan is for more to follow. The best so far is an installation called *Refugee*, by Pete Thornley, funded by the Arts Council in the West Midlands. Into a hole cut out of the ceiling of a large steel shipping container, a glass window has been inserted, inscribed with this quotation concerning the situation of refugees, that 'the sky is all that is left to appeal to in certain circumstances' (John Berger).

below: *Walking Monk,* by Lyell Arbs. Bronze resin. Exhibited in 2007. *Photo by Alison Stace.*
opposite: *Wings over Water,* by Walenty Pytel, 2000. Galvanised steel.

The Midlands

16 Coventry Canal Art Trail

Information:

(Urban Rangers' office), Culture & Leisure, Unit 6, Canal Basin, St Nicholas Street, Coventry, CV1 4LY.
Tel: 024 7678 5508
www.covcanalsoc.org.uk/art_trail.htm

Facilities: A little café in the canal basin and a couple of pubs along the way (by bridge No.7 and on Bedworth Rd, come up at bridge No.9). However, as it took about 2 ½ hours to walk the whole trail, you may want to take some lunch with you so you can stop wherever you find a bench. There are public toilets by bridge No.1, though these may no longer be in use.
Open: All year
Admission: Free
Time needed: 2 ½ hours

Getting there

By road

Approaching Coventry city centre along the A4600, follow signs for the ring road, which runs internally around the actual centre itself. From the ring road you will see brown signs for the Canal Basin. Follow these until they lead you onto Foleshill Road and then immediately direct you off to a left turn into Leicester Row. The car park on your left is open to the public at weekends. The canal starts here.

By train

Coventry station is on the other side of Coventry from the canal basin, but is still only a 10-minute walk. Alternatively, you can take a bus to the bus station (then a 5-minute walk).

Getting back

At the end of the walk, you can return to the canal basin by bus. Retrace your steps briefly back along the canal, passing back under bridge No.11, and the M6 motorway, then come up onto the road at bridge No.10. Turn left and walk along the road for a few minutes to Longford Church and square. There is a bus stop in front of the church. Take buses 20 or 50 from here (every 15 mins) to Ironmonger Row in Coventry. The bus takes about 10–15 minutes to Ironmonger Row (just off Trinity Street), which is a 5 to 10-minute walk back to the canal basin.

Overview

Running from Coventry city centre out as far as Hawkesbury Junction, the Coventry Canal Art Trail was set up in 1992. Some parts of the canal are very pretty, with trees, canal boats, little houses lining one side, ducks and swans; other parts go through bleak industrial areas, with disused factories and wasteland on either side. The idea of the sculpture trail was to re-generate the canal for the community, all on a limited budget. As a result, many of the works are forms of sculptural seating, and while some of the pieces on the trail are very inventive, others are uninspiring. There is often a fair distance between pieces, so the trail is more about walking the canal than looking at sculpture. You can buy a little booklet entitled '5 ½ Miles of Art' from the rangers' office (address on p.81 – open week-days, or order it in advance – £3), which gives an explanation of each piece. Or look at the map and details of work on their website. Although not the most exciting, the trail is one of the few community-art projects featuring sculptures, and it's also free, making art acces-sible in an urban environment. The project has been successful; a wide variety of people use the towpath, including boat owners, dog-walkers, cyclists, kids fishing and, inevitably, groups of boys drinking beer.

right: *James Brindley* by James Butler, 1998. Bronze, patinated dark brown.
far right: *Lady Scurrying* by Mark Tiley, approx. 1997. Galvanised steel, welded and forged. Located on Red Lane footbridge. *Photos by Alison Stace.*

The canal basin itself is very pretty. This is where the trail starts (the mosaic and sculp-ture of James Brindley can be found here), and the little café in the canal basin is a nice place to stop at the start or end of your walk.

There are a few nice pieces on the trail. The first is the bronze by James Butler of *James Brindley*, the engineer responsible in 1768 for the construction of the Coventry Canal. *Lady Scurrying*, by Mark Tilley, is a fantastic sculp-ture of a woman hurrying along in flowing shapes of galvanised metal. *Wings Over Water*, by Walenty Pytel makes a great end to the trail. The *Perch Seats* are colourful shapes of giant perch, bent into seats. These are a great example of an artist working with local children to produce something that really is original, funky and functional.

Finding your way around

The booklet is very informative, but towards the end the map becomes confused – in fact, the last sculptures are located at bridge 11, not 10 as the booklet indicates (the booklet is missing bridge 9). Along the walk, not all bridges are numbered (look for small metal plaques centrally placed on the brick), so you have to pay attention. Sometimes you need to come off the towpath onto a bridge to see a piece, and then continue back down. There is now a good map on the organisation's website which can be downloaded. You really can't get lost, but keep an eye on the map as you walk, as some of the sculptures are slightly hidden. The whole sculpture trail took about 2½ hours to walk. At bridge 11, the end of the trail, you need to retrace your steps back to bridge 10, where you can get a bus back to the canal basin (see instructions under 'Getting back').

17 Quenington Sculpture Trust

Fruit Drop Chandelier, by Neil Wilkin. Clear glass and stainless steel. Exhibited in 2007.

Information:

Quenington Old Rectory,
Quenington, Cirencester,
Gloucestershire, GL7 5BN
Tel: 01285 750358
www.freshairart.org

Facilities: Toilets & refreshments available
Open: One changing exhibition every year for a few weeks in June and July.
Admission: Free
Time needed: 1 ½ hours

Getting there

By road
From jct 15 of the M4, take A419, turn right onto A361, and left onto A417. • The A417 runs from Gloucester to Reading. • At Fairford, turn right (from Reading) or left (from Gloucester) towards Quenington and then follow signs to the exhibition.

Overview

The Quenington Sculpture Trust holds the 'Fresh Air' exhibition every other year, its aim being 'to educate, foster knowledge, understanding and appreciation of the arts'. 'Fresh Air 07' (their eighth show) displayed a range of media including bronze, ceramic, glass, metalwork, woven willow, marble and wire. The work was of a very high standard, and included some works on loan by very well-known artists such as Lynn Chadwick and Graham Williams. Some of the best glass pieces were by Neil Wilkins (also on show at Hannah Peschar, see p. 105), and there was also an unusual woven willow sculpture by Laura Ellen Bacon. The University of Gloucestershire art foundation course also provided some surprisingly good work, including a series of chairs emerging from the earth and heading out towards the river, and some morbid wax heads on poles. There was also a fabulous music installation, activated by people taking a seat under a lovely wooden pergola covered over with roses.

Although this is a selling show, it wasn't full of work on plinths: pieces are carefully sited to fit in with the beautiful gardens, which have both a river at one end and a small mill race running through to a sluice. It took about an hour and a half to wander round and see everything. Although each biennial exhibition is only on for a short time, Quenington is well worth a visit.

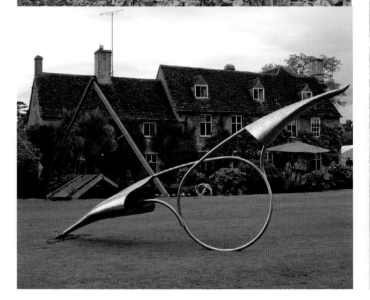

right above: *Floating Causeway*, by Kate Ivy-Williams from the University of Gloucestershire foundation course. Exhibited in 2007.
below: *The Quickening*, by Nicholas Uhlmann. Copper, stainless steel and aluminium. Exhibited in 2007.
opposite: *Fallow Buck and Fallow Doe*, by Miranda Michels. Mild steel.
Photos by Alison Stace, by permission of Quenington Sculpture Trust.

18 Chatsworth House & Gardens

Information:

Chatsworth, Bakewell, Derbyshire DE45 1PP.
Tel: 01246 583139
www.chatsworth.org

Facilities: Café, toilets, gift shop.
Open: mid-Mar–23 Dec (check for exact dates) (gardens only) 11am–6pm, (house) 11am–5.30pm
Admission (garden only): Adult £7.45, Concessions £5.80, Child £3.60, Family £16.50 (with house included approx. £4 extra). Parking £2.

Getting there

By road
Take M1 to jct 29, then A617 towards Chesterfield, then A619 towards Baslow & Bakewell. Then take B6012 towards Rowsley & follow brown signs.

By train
From Chesterfield station Chatsworth is a 30 to 40-minute bus ride then a 2-mile walk, or 25 minutes by taxi. From Sheffield station, 1 hour by bus or 30 mins by taxi.

right: *Walking Madonna*, by Dame Elisabeth Frink, 1981. *Photo by Alison Stace, courtesy of the Frink Estate.*

Overview

Chatsworth is not strictly a sculpture park, and does not promote itself as one at present. Nevertheless, it does have a few good sculptures. Originally established 450 years ago and adapted by various head gardeners since, the lovely gardens feature a huge cascading waterfall and a rock garden among other things. There are only 12 permanent contemporary sculptures, mostly modern British, but these are very good. Two more are due to be added to the collection in 2008, by Alan Jones and David Nash.

For the last two years they have also hosted an exhibition of sculpture in the grounds from September to November, called 'Beyond Limits' and organised by Sotheby's. In 2007, 23 spectacular pieces of modern and contemporary sculpture were displayed in the grounds by artists such as Rodin, Lynn Chadwick, Damien Hirst, Anish Kapoor and Mark Quinn. It is uncertain if this will become a regular feature (although it is certainly hoped that a regular exhibition will happen). If it does continue, the work will change each year and it is well worth combining your visit with this event (check website for details and time of year).

right: *War Horse*, by Dame Elisabeth Frink, 1991. *Photo by Alison Stace, courtesy of the Frink Estate.*

Things to see

In the permanent collection, there are three works by Dame Elisabeth Frink (from 1974, 1981 and 1991), and two by Barry Flanagan, the most recent of which is *Drummer*, added in 1996. Other notable pieces include *Lion Woman*, by Emily Young, from 1991 (her stone heads can also be seen at Hannah Peschar, see p.102); *Screen*, by Allen Young, featuring the shapes of figures in an almost 3D line drawing made from painted black stainless steel; *Figure of a Man* by William Turnbull (1988); and the latest piece, a water sculpture by Angela Conner, added in 1999. You could see everything in an hour and a half if you do not get lost in the maze, distracted by Joseph Paxton's amazing rock garden, or diverted by the treasures inside the house! You'll find a map showing locations of sculptures on the garden leaflet.

The South-east

- Greater London • Kent • East & West Sussex • Hampshire
- Surrey • Bedfordshire • Hertfordshire • Cambridgeshire
- Berkshire • Oxfordshire • Norfolk • Suffolk • Essex

19 Henry Moore
   Foundation
20 Cass Sculpture
   Foundation at
   Goodwood
21 Hannah Peschar
   Sculpture Garden
22 Pride of the Valley
   Sculpture Park

Other Places of Interest
23 Chiltern Sculpture Trail
24 Stour Valley Arts in
   King's Wood
25 Derek Jarman's Garden
26 'Art in the Garden' at
   Sir Harold Hillier's
   Gardens
27 The Garden Gallery
28 The Gibberd Garden
29 Bergh Apton Sculpture
   Trail

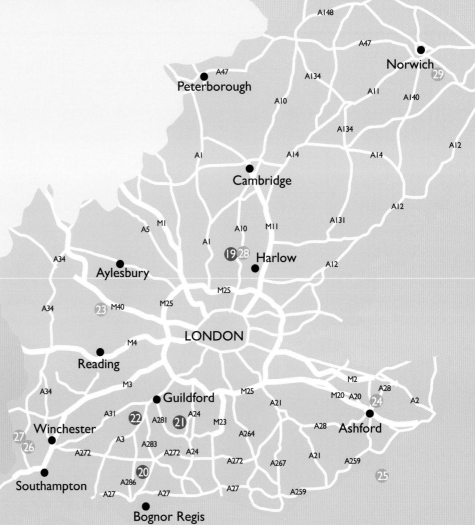

19 The Henry Moore Foundation

Information:

Dan Tree House, Perry Green, Much Hadham, Hertfordshire, SG10 6EE.
Tel: 01279 843333
www.henry-moore-fdn.co.uk

Facilities: There are toilets on site, but no café. However, virtually next door (a 2-min. walk) is the Hoops Inn, which has a beer garden and serves food (although, be warned, this can take some time).

Open: April–mid-Oct by appointment only. Before setting off make sure you ring in advance to arrange a visit. They are more than happy to accommodate visitors, but they avoid having them on days when cranes and lorries are arriving to move work, for obvious reasons.

Admission: (gardens & studios only) adults £7, concessions £5, students and under 18s free. (Add about £3 extra for combined ticket for tour of Hoglands.)

Time needed: 1 ½ – 2 hours

Sheep Piece, 1971–72 (LH 627). Bronze. Photo by Michael Phipps, reproduced by permission of the Henry Moore Foundation.

Getting there

By road

• Take M11 to jct 8, then take the A120 towards Hertford. • Go straight over two roundabouts and at the third follow signs for Much Hadham. • After 3 miles, turn left opposite Great Hadham Golf Course down a lane signposted to Green Tye (this suddenly appears around a corner). Cross straight over the next crossroads. • Go through Green Tye into Perry Green, bearing left at the church (the road curves round it). • Continue for about ¼ mile to a green with a telephone box on the left. The Henry Moore Foundation is signposted on the green.

By train

To Bishop's Stortford then taxi to Perry Green (approx. 15 minutes). (Trains run from Liverpool Street Station, London).

Double Oval, 1966 (LH 560). Bronze.
Double Oval (detail), 1966 (LH 560). Bronze.
Photos by Michael Phipps, reproduced by permission of the Henry Moore Foundation.

Overview

Henry Moore (1898–1986) lived here from 1951 until his death in 1986, and began by moving into the house, known as Hoglands, and gradually buying up other bits of land and buildings as they became available. In 1977 he gave the estate to the Foundation. The final estate covered 70 acres with various different studios being used for specific things. Moore's house is now being restored and should also be open to the public in the spring of 2008.

Moore is perhaps the most widely exhibited British sculptor, and all exhibitions of his work are coordinated from here. Therefore at any given time certain pieces may have been

each piece, many of the pieces having been sited by Moore himself.

As well as the beautiful and very spacious grounds, the various studios are open to visitors and remain much as they were left. The White Studio was built in the 1950s for making the plaster moulds, and the Yellow Brick Studio, used by Moore for carving in, now holds several pieces in marble and plaster, and also has a very useful video and models of the lost-wax method of bronze casting for those interested in the technical aspects of his work. The Aisled Barn (a relocated medieval structure) and the Sheep Field Barn are used to display textiles and changing exhibitions. My personal favourite, however, is the Bourne Maquette Studio, which was built in 1970 to house the ever-growing collection of natural found objects gathered by Moore over 30 years, which he used sometimes for inspiration and sometimes as the actual starting point of a maquette. As well as modelling simply in plaster or clay, he would take a small stone or piece of driftwood that suggested a shape to him, and add to it with plaster or clay. For me this fascinating assortment of strange objects gave a clear insight into his work, and seemed more illuminating than many of his drawings.

The Foundation also has a library and archive which serious students can ask to use. Anyone interested can make an appointment in advance with the very helpful librarian, Michael Phipps.

loaned out (for example, the Yorkshire Sculpture Park always has a few pieces), though there will always be a good selection of his work to be seen in the well-kept grounds.

Henry Moore is famous for his large-scale bronze sculptures, but is less well-known for his printmaking, drawings, lithography and textiles. In view of this, a show featuring his textiles is planned for the Sheep Field Barn Gallery at the Foundation in 2008/9.

The sculpture and the grounds are not really that big (most of the 70 acres are unused fields). Everything in the grounds has been well placed to allow lots of space around

Finding your way around

The sculptures are all well sited, and the grounds are very carefully maintained (but wear walking shoes, as a couple of the large pieces are located in a very muddy field). Much of the land that was not used during Moore's lifetime has now been made accessible to visitors to enable more works to be displayed. It is possible to see quite a few pieces while sticking solely to the paths, but you can't always get up close. The continuous programme of loans to other exhibitions means the map given out to visitors is changed about every six months. The map numbers the pieces and locates them within the grounds for you, but there is no recommended route for viewing them. It took us about an hour and a half to see everything – although if you want to study the indoor exhibitions more closely, it could take much longer.

left: *Knife Edge Two Piece*, 1962–65, (LH 516). *Photo by Michael Phipps, reproduced by permission of the Henry Moore Foundation.*
right: *The Arch*, 1969 (LH 503b). *Photo by Suzanne Eustace, reproduced by permission of the Henry Moore Foundation.*

Things to see

As the sculptures are prone to being moved around, and many have the same or similar names and themes, I have also included the catalogue number (LH number) to make it clear which piece is being discussed. As always with sculpture parks, not everything mentioned will necessarily be on display. Sadly, there is now one piece permanently missing piece from the collection, *Reclining Figure* (LH 608), which was stolen by professional art thieves in December 2005 and has so far not been traced.

Large Figure in a Shelter (1985/6, LH652c) is one sculpture that hardly ever moves, purely because the cost of moving such an enormous work is prohibitive. This giant bronze has the most intense colour, and its very definite edges emphasise the form. It becomes obvious from the title that the person underneath the cut-open form is sheltering, and is a variation on a theme Moore often worked with of internal/external shapes, which link to ideas of body/spirit, mother/baby, protective shell and soft internal being. Moore often revisited themes, one of which was the 'Helmet Heads', which began in the 1950s and developed over the next 30 years. *Large Figure in a Shelter* is often seen as the final piece on this theme.

A cast of *Knife Edge Two Piece* (1962–5, LH516) stands outside the Houses of Parliament (this is the original) and is often used as a backdrop by reporters. This piece is par-

ticularly striking because the view of it changes radically as you walk around it, so that side on the two pieces seem as if they are very sharp and angular – the knife edge – while straight on they appear wide and flat. It almost looks like two separate sculptures. The careful balance of this large, heavy form with the fine edge forces you to think more closely about the appearance of forms and the nature of three dimensions. Moore chose the site for this work very carefully – it can be seen from the back of Hoglands.

Double Oval (1966, LH560) is my current favourite work by Moore. This sculpture is a set of two forms, and one seems to echo the other, although Moore's dislike of symmetry makes them unlikely to be identical.

The use of the hole to pierce the form, begun in the 1930s, is here taken to extremes. The sculpture is as much hole as form, opening the forms right up, and the elegant shapes change dramatically as you walk around them.

It is clear from the title what is represented by *Three Piece Sculpture: Vertebrae* (1968, LH580). The inspiration and the forms are obviously organic bones, but having been enlarged so much they lose their natural context and become simply abstract shapes. They work so amazingly well together, however, that walking round you get an ever-changing assortment of forms. The golden colour of the bronze comes from a lacquer intended to weatherproof the surface.

Goslar Warrior (1973–74, LH641) was made by Moore as a commission for the town of Goslar in Germany, the result of winning a prestigious art prize. He had made several previous warriors in the 1950s, and had returned to the theme around 1970. Each one has elements of tragedy, defiance and resignation in varied amounts, as they fight or die despite injuries and missing limbs. The warrior figure was thus something he developed gradually over many years, with the result that this one seems to be the resigned summation of all the others. Some of the warriors have a missing arm or a missing leg; this one has no limbs beside the leg that the shield rests against.

Large Reclining Figure (LH192b) is located dramatically on top of a hill that looks as if it was built specifically for the purpose, and in fact it was; originally a pyramid of gravel, Moore got a bulldozer to flatten it off, creating the perfect location. This piece was commissioned by the architect I.M. Pei for the Chinese Bank in Singapore. The top half and bottom half are almost separate works – but the arms seem to join and steady the whole piece, drawing it together. This figure was enlarged in 1983 from a tiny maquette made in 1938.

above left: *Three Piece Sculpture: Vertebrae* (detail), 1968. *Photo by Alison Stace, reproduced by permission of the Henry Moore Foundation.*
right: *Large Figure in a Shelter*, 1985–86. *Photo from The Henry Moore Foundation Archive.*

20 Cass Sculpture Foundation at Goodwood

Information:

Sculpture Estate, Goodwood, West Sussex,
PO18 0QP.
Tel: 01243 538 449
www.sculpture.org.uk

Facilities: Unexpectedly for such a large and
high-profile park, there are no facilities
other than some toilets in the deer hut
(about halfway round), but as always several
trusty British pubs serving food can be
found in nearby villages.
Open: Apr–Oct, Tue–Sun (& Bank Holiday
Mondays), 10.30am–5pm.
Admission: Adults £10, children under 10
free with adult (separate conditions for
school groups).
Time needed: 2 ½ hours

right: *I'm Alive* by Tony Cragg, 2005. Stainless steel.
far right: (left) *Tongue in Cheek* by Tony Cragg,
2002. Bronze. (Right) *Declination* by Tony Cragg,
2005. Yellow bronze.
Photos courtesy of Cass Sculpture Foundation.

Getting there

By road

The estate is well signposted, so if in doubt follow brown signs to Goodwood House until you see signs for Sculpture at Goodwood.

From the north, take the A3 south, and turn left onto A283 to Petworth. • At Petworth take the A285 towards Chichester. • After going through Duncton, turn right towards Goodwood racecourse/Singleton and follow the road for about 2 miles until you reach a small crossroads. Turn left between two lodge gates, and the sculpture estate is 1 mile down the road on the left.

From the south, take the A285 towards Petworth, follow signs to Goodwood Motor Circuit, and after passing it on your left, at the next roundabout take the third exit for the Marriott Hotel (ignore signs to racecourse here). • Take the next left and follow the road past the hotel up the hill. The sculpture estate is on the right.

By train

Take the Portsmouth Harbour/Bognor Regis line to Barnham (trains run from Victoria, London), or a train on the Brighton/Portsmouth line to Barnham. From Barnham station its about 10 mins by taxi.

Overview

Goodwood is one of the very well-known, high-profile sculpture parks. It is very well maintained and run to an impressively high, although not always very friendly, level of efficiency. The Foundation is a registered charity, set up specifically to promote and exhibit British sculpture. The extensive grounds are home to a vast number of large and impressive sculptures by well-known sculptors. The idea is to engage the public and display works for public viewing, although works are also sold or loaned out on a part-time basis. Thus, as with most

parks, the work does change, opening up space for new commissions. Goodwood is one of the best places to go to see work by the most prominent and established artists (along with Yorkshire Sculpture Park and Roche Court). One whole area has been devoted just to Tony Cragg in the largest exhibition of his outdoor work so far. Each piece is perfectly positioned in the landscaped grounds to show it at it's best.

On arrival, head for the large reception and visitors' gallery, to pay admission and be given a guide to the sculptures on show in the park. The gallery was designed by award-winning architects Studio Downie, who also designed the impressive Foundation Centre in the heart of the park, though this is not open to the public.

Finding your way around

The estate is very large, with many open areas, although much of the park is located in wooded areas which provided a shady relief on the scorching-hot day we visited. It took us about 2½ hours to see everything (approx. 70 sculptures), though this did involve a certain amount of backtracking to reach a hidden piece (as per the instructions), so nothing was missed. Goodwood uses a set of instructions combined with colour images of all the works to guide you round the park (the same system as at Hannah Peschar), which works very well. It helps to see what you are looking for next and, if you stray from the directions, to locate yourself again by the images of work. When things become more confused in the woods towards the end (with sculptures listed as 'through the trees' and paths leading off in every direction), a bright-yellow wiggly arrow stuck in the ground often points you in the right direction. But be warned – in the woods towards the end of the sculpture park route, some of the paths lead up to the private house and are barred only by a few small signs. On the day we visited some unfortunate visitors overlooked the signs and set off a very loud alarm, causing Foundation staff to come scurrying.

far left: *Fish on a Bicycle,* by Steven Gregory, 1998. Bronze.
left: *Kiss,* by Billy Lee. Granite.
right: *Regardless of History,* by Bill Woodrow, 2000. Bronze.
Photos courtesy of Cass Sculpture Foundation.

Things to see

The standard of work at Goodwood is very high, and it is hard not to appreciate the thought and careful creation of most pieces even if you don't personally like them all.

Directly in front of the visitors' gallery, *Sylla II*, by William Pye, I found utterly captivating. An incredibly simple combination of an acrylic tube filled with water and a twisting mechanism at the bottom, the effect was a speeded-up process of water wanting to drain down a plughole, but, not being able to escape, squeezing upwards into an ever-tighter rising spiral.

One of my favourite pieces was Anthony Abrahams's *Walking*, which looked even better as you walked around it and saw the two figures united in their perfect symmetry yet heading in opposite directions. Further down the hill was Bill Woodman's *Regardless of History*. This enormous sculpture shows a huge metal tree growing over and out of a giant pile of books and a tomb, conveying the message that time and nature neither wait nor care for any man.

The display of Anthony Gormley's work was disappointing – simply because the pieces we had hoped to see had been sold and nothing

had yet arrived to replace them. This is one of the hazards of sculpture parks – things change and move about. However, though there are always a couple of disappointments, these are usually swept aside by some unexpected discoveries. In this case, there was a large area put aside for Tony Cragg which certainly did not disappoint. The area has been carefully landscaped to show various sculptures at their best. My favourites were two carved and twisting sculptures, *Here Today Gone Tomorrow* and *Bent of Mind*. *Here Today Gone To-*

morrow consists of two columns made of stone whose haunting, unbalanced forms seem to have been naturally formed by a sandstorm. Eerie faces appear and disappear as you get closer or walk around the twisting columns. *Bent of Mind* is a bronze in the same style, but this one piece has two faces on opposite sides, whose misshapen features look like nature's true forms trying to escape from the metal. Cragg's nearby silver sculpture entitled *I'm Alive* I found both creepy and moving, resembling as it did a hybrid of both a threatening shark out of water and a tortured life form. It looks both familiar and alien, at the same time both a plea for help and a threat. Further along the path leading out of this area is Cragg's *Tongue in Cheek*, a bronze form with pierced walls, which offers a teasing play on words and ideas, as the shapes turn themselves inside out and fit one inside the other.

There were a couple of interactive pieces that really engaged us: Gavin Turk's *Golden Thread*, an aluminium and glass maze, which you walk through seeing both your own reflected image in the glass and at the same time (in the summer) a beautiful field of poppies beyond; and William Furlong's visually unassuming *Walls of Sound*, towards the end of the park, more aural experience than aesthetic object. Made up of two walls of steel, the piece invites you to walk along the narrow alley between them while sounds of a tropical jungle are played along with some faint music. The effect is brilliant, and ties in really well with the

surroundings, as all you can see are the walls and the trees overhead.

Steven Gregory has several sculptures in the park, but for me the most impressive of his works was the *Samurai Warrior*, an amazing bronze which looks like a cross between origami and a shadow puppet. The whole figure seems to have been cut out of a giant piece of bronze sheeting, and then rearranged and pushed through to make it 3D. It simply has to be seen to be comprehended.

Other large-scale works worth mentioning include Stephen Cox's *Granite Catamarans on a Granite Wave*, which genuinely captures the sense of movement of boats at sea – impressive for something made of granite.

Towards the end was Peter Burke's *Register*, a whole collection of seemingly rusted hands, it had unnerving associations with Auchwitz, and was both eerie and moving.

Finally, not to be missed is Sean Henry's *Lying Man*, resting on its own specially built mound of earth. Unusually made of bronze painted with oils, this fantastically realistic and larger-than-life sculpture of Sean Henry seems perfectly at home. Compare this version of him to the one at the Hannah Peschar Sculpture Garden, where he can be spotted striding along beside a hedge.

far left: *Granite Catamarans on a Granite Wave* by Stephen Cox, 1994. Black and white granite.
left: *Stairway*, by Danny Lane, 2007.
Photos courtesy of Cass Sculpture Foundation.

21 Hannah Peschar Sculpture Garden

Information:

Black & White Cottage, Standon Lane,
Ockley, Surrey, RH5 5QR.
Tel: 01306 627269
www.hannahpescharsculpture.com

Facilities: None at Hannah Peschar, but
some good pubs serving lunch (usually
12–3pm) and coffee in the village of Ockley,
so time your visit accordingly.
Open: May–Oct, Fri & Sat 11am–6pm, Sun &
Bank Hols 2–5pm, Tue–Thu (no concessions)
by appointment; Nov–Apr by appointment
only.
Admission: Adults £9, children £6,
concessions £7.
Time needed: 2 hours

Getting there

By road

Take A24 (which runs from near Worthing up
to Ewell), and turn at Beare Green onto the
A29 towards Ockley. At Ockley, turn into
Cathill Lane by The Old School House pub,
then turn left at the end into Standon Lane.
Once over the bridge, the entrance is on
your right. Pay close attention in order to
spot the green sign against the green trees.

By train:

Ockley train station then 10 mins by taxi.

Overview

This stunning garden is amongst the most established and renowned of the sculpture gardens, its beautifully arranged grounds matched by a high standard of sculpture. The varied selection of work has been carefully positioned to bring out the best in both sculpture and surroundings. The garden is also one of the few to show a good range of glass sculpture. It operates as an outdoor gallery, with exhibits for sale, so work is always changing.

The garden started life as part of an estate laid out between 1915 and 1920, which was later sold off in parts. Hannah Peschar bought a neglected 10-acre section of the original garden, including the 15th-century cottage, and over the last 24 years the garden has been redesigned and gradually nurtured back to life by landscape designer Anthony Paul. The twisting moss-covered paths lead you through wooded areas and alongside the many ponds, which are fringed by unusual giant-leaved plants and colourful flowers. A fairytale ambience pervades this garden, with its little wooden bridges across the ponds, hidden paths and clearings, and Hansel and Gretel-style tiny wooden lodges tucked away amongst the trees.

far left: *Winged Angel,* by Emily Young.
left: *In the Balance,* by Laurence Edwards. Bronze. *Photos courtesy of Hannah Peschar Sculpture Garden.*

Finding your way around

A leaflet with small pictures, which you can get at reception, guides you around every sculpture in the garden, giving instructions on where to turn and which path to follow. The images help you to orientate yourself if you lose the thread. The garden at first glance looks quite small, but this is deceptive, as the paths weave their way into hidden areas which continually open out and lead on to further spaces – allow a couple of hours.

above: *Sky Surf* by Rick Kirby. Stainless steel on mild steel. *Photo courtesy of Hannah Peschar Sculpture Garden.*

Things to see

Hannah Peschar operates as an outdoor gallery, meaning work comes and goes and moves around. The following pieces were those that stood out at the time of visiting, though featured artists will often replace work sold with something similar.

Amongst the many fabulous glass sculptures, Neil Wilkin had several installed that worked particularly well with the environment, particularly *Cat Tails* and *Dew Drops*, both situated at the edge of a pond, reflecting light off the water and resembling majestic, shining aquatic plants. His *Red Fountain*, although not in operation,

offered a sumptuous splash of colour against the green and brown pond. Be sure also to see Matthew Durran's *Migration*, recreating the blur of a flock of birds in flight across the surface of the water. Simple yet stunning, it ties in superbly with its situation. On the other side of this pond is *Leaning-Straight-Leaning*, by Bert Frijns, looking like nothing more than three giant, slightly skewed glasses of water. These glimmer from afar and are even more fascinating up close, as the pond reeds are magnified through the water in the glass as you move around them.

There is also a fair amount of figurative

sculpture to be found here. Graham Clayton's *Fragment*, a bronze broken head, lies in the grass like an undiscovered remnant from a lost civilization, while hidden away at the back of the garden lies another head, this time of giant proportions, Rick Kirby's *Broadside*, made from steel with an orange hue that is very striking in the green surroundings (see p.2–3). This enormous mask is hollow, its empty eyes allowing glimpses of sky and greenery to peak through, giving you the eerie feeling of looking at the death mask of a giant. Sean Henry's *Walking Man*, meanwhile, is so realistic that we both jumped when we caught sight of his head floating above the hedge. On further investigation, on the other side of the hedge we found a larger-than-life-size figure in resin, fully dressed and striding purposefully along a path. No doubt he is striding towards the Cass Sculpture Foundation at Goodwood, where he can also be found having a nap. Another figurative work worth noting is Emily Young's *Siena Torso*. While nearly all her pieces are lovely, this one is particularly striking, as she has managed to combine simplicity

above: *Broadside,* by Rick Kirby. Mild steel.
left: *Dewdrops,* by Neil Wilkins. Glass and stainless steel.
far left: *Leaning-Straight-Leaning* by Bert Frijns. Glass and water. *Photos courtesy of Hannah Peschar Sculpture Garden.*

The South-east

of form that balances well with the beauty and striking colour of the marble.

Imitating and reflecting nature, Beate Schroedl's *Bamboo with Discs* managed both to bring out and enhance the beauty of bamboo, while *Natural Circumference*, by Dominique Bivar Segurado, framed a circle of garden with what looks like actual pieces of stone, but is in fact stoneware clay. By using a natural material in a manmade shape, she has joined the two worlds of man and nature.

Amongst the larger pieces of work, there were three that particularly stood out. Walter Bailey's *Journey Work* I found very striking as well as unusual. This is made from large monolithic slices of oak stood at intervals with holes in them. Through these holes, from block to block, carved wooden pieces weave and wind, evoking wooden spirits finding their path through the holes in the oak until they reach the end, and then soaring up into the trees. Symbolically, the piece is made of raw and scorched wood. The second sculpture, quite different to the others, is the hard-to-miss *Changing Space* by George Cutts, made from long, bent stainless-steel poles that revolve electronically, turning and twisting. At first unconvinced, after a while I found this tranquil piece utterly mesmerising – the spaces and shapes created by the two poles resemble two swans locked in a complex, silent dance. Finally, be sure to see the enormous bronze *Hollow Dog*, by Maurice Blik, which guards the path in a slightly menacing fashion as you arrive and leave the car park.

22 THE PRIDE OF THE VALLEY SCULPTURE PARK

Information:

Jumps Rd, Churt, Farnham, Surrey,
GU10 2LE.
Tel: 01482 605453
www.thesculpturepark.com

Facilities: None in the park, though the Pride of the Valley Inn opposite serves very good food, and has a nice beer garden. The entrance to the sculpture park is through the small gate just opposite the pub, but the actual reception is a large wooden shed situated a little way inside the park (follow the small signposts on entering).
Opening: Tue–Sun, 10am–5pm, closed Mon (except Bank Hols).
Admission: Adults £6, children & senior citizens £3, under 5s free.
Time needed: 2-3 hours

far left: *Walking* Man by Sean Henry, at the Hannah Peschar Sculpture Garden. Resin prototype. *Photo courtesy of Hannah Peschar Sculpture Garden.*
left: *Two Worlds* by Martyn Barrett, 2002. Stone. *Photo by Eddie Powell.*

The South-east

Getting there

Finding this park was a little tricky – but provided you are on the A287 and ask for Churt if lost, you can't go far wrong.

By road

From the direction of Hindhead on the A287, which runs between Farnham and Hindhead, turn right onto Jumps Road after the shop Miscellanea – the shop is easy to miss, but is on your right after the crossroads at the Devil's Punchbowl . At the end of Jumps Road, turn left into Tilford Road. On the corner is the park, conveniently located opposite the Pride of the Valley Inn.

From Farnham direction, again on the A287, just after you pass Frensham Great Pond and Pond Lane on your right, turn left onto Jumps Road. (If you miss this turning and find yourself on Old Brick Kiln Lane, driving to the end of this road and turning right will bring you onto Jumps Road.) At the end of Jumps Road, turn left into Tilford Road. On the corner is the park, opposite the Pride of the Valley Inn.

By train

Farnham station and 10 minutes by taxi.

right: *Speed Skaters* by Michael Marriot, 2003. Resin.
middle: *Alma en Pena* by Ramon Conde, 1998. Bronze, 1 of an edition of 6.
far right: *Rolling Horse* by Lucy Kinsella, 2004. Bronze. *Photos by Eddie Powell.*

Overview

Eddie Powell, an artist himself, opened this park in 2003, and runs it as a business (most work is for sale, although some pieces are permanent) along with the help of his gardener/technician and handyman Nick. The areas in the park vary a great deal: some open spaces have enormous pieces while other paths and terraced areas have lots of smaller sculptures. In a similar way to the Hannah Peschar Sculpture Garden, this park looks deceptively small yet continuously opens out into bigger areas. Unlike Hannah

Peschar, the gardens are very much left wild and unkempt, although obviously the paths and the spaces around sculptures are all kept clear. There are small paths around the lake, winding through enormous bushes, over ponds, into wooded areas and up bankings, often going back and forth through an area so that you see the same piece from

the back as you go past again. There are sculptures everywhere (at the last visit 184), and often the sheer quantity of the work combined with all the vegetation around is a bit overwhelming, making it hard to concentrate on individual pieces. As my friend commented, it was a bit like going through someone's cluttered attic and finding treasures in amongst everything else. However, although a bit too crowded for me, this is also part of its appeal – the sculptures vary massively in style and are tucked away everywhere you look. There is certainly something to suit every taste, and the materials used also vary greatly, to include bronze, glass, wood, stone, even glass wax. The variety of work will certainly keep children entertained while exploring – but remember to keep them under supervision.

The park is big enough to house many enormous pieces of work, and if you like your sculptures big, then this is the place for you. But make sure, if you want to see everything, that you have the time and energy to devote to the search. Alternatively, if you are just interested in a nice day out, then a random stroll looking at whatever catches your eye would be an approach well suited to this park. Eddie Powell says with dramatic finality, 'The park is now full', and then undermines himself by promptly following it up with 'unless it's a really good one'. So having filled his seven acres he is now (trying) to be much more rigorous in selecting new pieces. Work changes as pieces are sold.

Finding your way around

The trail is about a mile and a half, and takes most people 2–3 hours, but as always this depends on the speed you walk at and how many things you stop to look at properly. The park has printed directions to help you navigate the paths, and a colour-coded system has been worked out according to the length of route and the time it will take to go round. Different coloured wiggly arrows point the way depending on which route you follow. It works quite well providing you keep a close eye on which way you are going. Broadly speaking, the yellow and red routes take you around the perimeter, while the blue and green routes are the inside of the park. The yellow and red arrows eventually bring you back past the reception part-way through anyhow, so if you are short of time you can always stop at this point.

Things to see

There was so much to see at Pride of the Valley that it's hard to narrow down the list to just a few. However, in the biggest part of the park, in the grassy open area, there are some larger-than-life sculptures, such as the *Rolling Horse*, made in bronze by Lucy Kinsella, which vividly conveys both movement and joy. Her *Fighting Hares* once located at the entrance are also impressive and dramatic, and look out for her other pieces, most recently of a gorilla and a baboon.

I was very taken with a line of larger-than-life cartwheeling wooden figures by Sophie Dickens, though I did feel that the piece needed more space around it in order to be fully appreciated – they were somewhat hemmed in by other less impressive works, making it hard to see properly. The wooden versions of these figures are now being cast in bronze. (Look out for figures climbing a tree by the same artist). Also in this area are *The Four Horses of the Apocalypse* by Anthony Haywood, a superbly inventive piece made out of recycled materials – including everything from old dolls and telephones to plastic bottles. I thought these were great – though sadly they have been partly eroded by unruly children – and are starting to lose their form.

left: *The Brockhall Warrior* by Joanna Malin-Davies, 2003. Jesmonite.
above: *Rolling Horse* by Lucy Kinsella, 2004. Bronze.

The *Cork Eagle* by Robert Bradford, hidden amongst the trees on a hillside, is quite an astounding size, although not one of the best pieces. It was commissioned by the RSPB to draw attention to the fact that the wine industry is switching over to plastic corks. The cork forests in Spain are also the habitat of eagles and other creatures, and with the decline of traditional wine-bottle corks are now in danger. On close inspection you can see that the bird's underside is constructed from hundreds of corks attached to a steel framework.

Near the start of the park, the *Circus Elephants*, made from welded-together sheets of metal, were impressive from their almost life-size scale alone, and another giant piece, very close to the elephants, was an enormous *Spider* by Wilfred Pritchard, made from flat pieces interlocked, which managed to enthral and menace simultaneously.

On the lake are the very vivid and eye-catching *Speed Skaters*, which have the look of cartoon characters and are very cleverly weighted down just enough to be caught by the wind and thus constantly moving across the water, appearing to skate.

Another enjoyable piece was the surreal blue figure with an umbrella, *Lady with*

Umbrella, by Ofra Zimbalista. It wasn't clear whether the column below her was holding her back as she tried to float away in a Mary-Poppins style, or whether it was keeping her up in the air. In contrast, the mournful-looking *Dame Kind*, by Sean Crampton, holds her arm out for a bird of prey and is both expressive and considered. Meanwhile,

in the bushes, a naked *Perseus* by Andrew Langley lunges forward with shield held aloft and sword in hand. This piece has tremendous movement and emotion. The heroic figure started life as polished steel, but I feel that the slightly rusty quality he has acquired with age better suits his rugged character.

above: *Giant Tarantula* by Wilfred Pritchard, 2005. Cor-Ten™ steel.

Other Places of Interest

23 Chiltern Sculpture Trail

Information:

Cowleaze Wood, Cowleaze, Buckinghamshire.
www.chilternsculpturetrail.co.uk

No facilities, but Fox and Hounds pub
nearby at Christmas Common.
Open: All year in daylight
Admission: Free
Time needed: 2 hours

Getting there

By road
Leave M40 at Jctn 5 and follow signs to the
A40 north towards Oxford for a mile. Turn
off the A40 at the television mast, following
signposts to the sculpture trail and Christmas Common and continue for 2 miles,
past the nature reserve, over the motorway
and Cowleaze is on the left. • Park in the
car park and look for the start of the trail –
an enormous concrete post visible from the
road, painted lime green and white.

By train
Nearest station is Saunderton, and taxi ride
of approx. 30 mins.

Fish Tree by Paul Amey, 1990. Steel and cast resin.
Photo by Alison Stace.

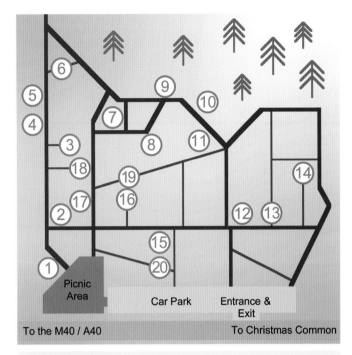

Chiltern Sculpture Trail

Picnic Area – Benches by Fred Baier, 1996. Painted steel.
– Info Post: Untitled (Chilterns) by Tom Woolford, 2002. Cast concrete.

1   Untitled by Miranda Peake, 2003. Wood and plastic.
2   **Rural Industry** by Sophie Horton, 1990. Handmade bricks and forest floor.
3   **Posts Modern** by Ally Wallace, 2003. Painted steel.
4   **A Platform for Self-Elevation** by Jonathan Griffin, 2001. Laminated wood.
5   **Ridgeback** by Stuart Turner, 2004. Hazel and willow.
6   **Fish Tree** by Paul Amey, 1990. Steel and cast resin.
7   **The In-between** by Alison Gill, 2005. Encapsulated fluorescent paper.
8   **Touching Earth and Sky** by Judith Cowan, 1991. Bronze.
9   **Reservoir of Gods** by Faisal Abdu'Al-lah, 1999. Concrete and stainless steel.
10 **Copper Beech** by George Mogg, 2004. Coins and copper wire.
11 **This is the Future** by Bram Arnold,
2003. Sand, bricks, tarmac and paint.
12 **Southern Electric** by Louise K. Wilson, 2002. Earth mound, stainless steel and power lines.
13 **Coming Ready or Not** by Chloe Brown, 2000. Telegraph pole and loudspeaker.
14 **My Frozen Hand** by Rui Chafes, 1994. Painted steel.
15 **Techniques of the Bird Observer** by Rosemarie McGoldrick, 2006. Muto-scope viewer.
16 Untitled by Thomas Eisl, 1992. Wing mirrors.
17 **Nature Girl** by Laura Ford, 1993. Painted bronze.
18 Untitled by Hideo Futura, 1990. Pink granite.
19 **Above and Below** by Andrew Sabin, 1994. Black paint and strapping.
20 **Heimat II** by Roger Perkins, 1991. Tin, wood, steel and toys.

Other temporary works may also be installed.

right: *Nature Girl*, by Laura Ford, 1993. Painted bronze.
middle: *Reservoir of Gods*, by Faisal Abdu'Allah, 1999. Concrete and stainless steel.
far right: *Above and Below*, by Andrew Sabin, 1994. Black paint and strapping.

Overview

Cowleaze Wood is a surprisingly beautiful and somewhat creepy location for this sculpture trail, which was set up by a charitable organisation and is run by volunteers on a part-time basis. The idea was to generate interest and discussion in what outdoor art should be, and pieces vary wildly both in content and quality. The trail was set up in 1990 and is a collaboration with the Forestry Commission, and while many pieces remain, other pieces are only on display for a year or so.

One of the good things about the trail is that artists have been encouraged to do site-specific works, and some of the conceptual pieces are amongst the best. Signs along the way by Miranda Peake

give eerie reminders of horror movies, and work really well, with phrases such as 'Darling it's getting dark now' and 'I'll wait right here'. Another conceptual piece was an enormous megaphone rigged up on a post and aimed at the forest, by Chloe Brown, entitled *Coming Ready or Not*, suggesting an enormous game of hide-and-seek in the forest. Other interesting pieces included the *Reservoir of Gods* by Faisal Abdu'Allah featuring stainless-steel images of people on concrete posts, some looking challengingly at the camera, and others with their head in their hands. *Nature Girl* by Laura Ford is a bronze statue of a limbless tree trunk with tiny child's legs and red shoes – this piece looked great in its setting – a literal hybrid of mankind and forest. The *Fish Tree* by Paul Amey was surreal in its realistic creation, and the mutoscope viewer of a rare bird in flight spotted in the forest (by Rosemarie McGoldrick) was great to watch and relevant to its location.

The trail has several paths, as well as pieces off the main trail on smaller paths, and it took us 2 hours to go around. The map of sculptures provided by the website is a bit sketchy and some pieces we never found – although this could be because the pieces had disintegrated over time and been removed. A pleasant walk in a lovely setting with some interesting pieces to hunt out, making for a nice afternoon's outing. I would recommend going with a friend as the wood can be very quiet and the smaller paths a little confusing.

24 Stour Valley Arts In King's Wood

Information:

Information only:
Stour Valley Arts, King's Wood Forest Office,
Buck Street, Challock, Kent, TN25 4AR
Tel: 01233 740040
www.stourvalleyarts.org

Facilities: None but there is a nice pub
with a garden called the Halfway House at
Challock
Open: All year
Admission: Free
Time needed: 2½ hours

Getting there

By road
Exit the M20 at jct 8 onto the A20 towards
Harrietsham. At Challock turn right at the
crossroads onto the A251, then first left
(signposted King's Wood). The car park is
on your left.

By train & bus
Faversham station and Bus no.666 from
station, or Ashford station then bus no.666
from Park Street. Or from Canterbury station then bus no.667 from bus station.

right: *Coppice Cloud Chamber* by Chris Drury,
1998. *Photo by Alison Stace.*
far right: *Score for a Hole in the Ground (detail),*
by Jem Finer, 2006. *Photo by Alison Stace.*

Overview

King's Wood is a large forest – 1500 acres – with a sculpture trail that has been open

since 1994. (It sounds huge, but in fact the trail is only 3½ miles long and takes about two and a half hours to walk.) Stour Valley Arts commission all sorts of artworks including photographs, pieces of music and films, some of which are performed or shown in the forest for short periods. The forest is beautiful, and the walking very nice, but the sculptures vary a great deal, and the map (which can be downloaded from their website) is quite confusing. The trail is essentially a big loop, though it is not immediately clear which way round you should go, and it took us longer than expected to find our way around and locate works. The trail is marked by posts with green footprints. There are 12 works marked on the trail, but some of them are off the beaten path along small tracks, and some have fallen apart over time, so they can be hard to find. Look hard for the posts that point to artworks – extremely unobtrusive wooden fence posts with small bronze plaques. The play and picnic area has some fantastic insect-shaped seating for lunch with children.

Before you visit, it is worth looking at the 'commissions' page on the website for more thorough background information on current sculptures, especially as some are more complicated than they first appear (such as Score for a Hole in the Ground, which has won several awards), and others are somewhat obscure.

Things to see

There were a couple of pieces by Richard Harris that we never found, but eventually we realised that the large open flat area is the outdoor studio. Also, the long and odd-looking ballet rail/fence is The Last Eleven Years by Peter Fillingham, which does not separate anything from anything else, but winds its way through the trees to nowhere in particular. The best sculpture, in my opinion, was Coppice Cloud Chamber, by Chris Drury, which looks like a little wooden hut, made with all the logs stacked in a domelike shape with their ends pointing out. Through the small doorways inside you come into a dark chamber, with only a tiny hole in the ceiling letting light in, acting as a camera obscura. Once your eyes become accustomed to the light it's actually lovely. The roof has also been constructed very carefully using small planks in a square formation.

Nearby is Jem Finer's Score for a Hole in the Ground, comprised of one enormous horn and, opposite, the hole in the ground. This is actually a very subtle musical piece, depending on good conditions and your patience to listen. There were two quite obscure sculptures – both in location and content. Lukasz Skapski's Via Lucem Continens is an avenue of yews planted in alignment with the sunset on the longest day of the year, the date of an annual picnic now held to observe it. B52, by Rosie Leventon, is a cleared area of forest floor in the shape of a B52 bomber.

The South-east

25 Derek Jarman's Garden

Information:

Prospect Cottage, Dungeness, Kent.

Facilities: None.
Admission: Free (private garden)

right: Daffodils in Spring. *Photo courtesy of Keith Collins.*
far right: Sculptural arrangement of old anti-tank fencing posts. *Photo by Alison Stace.*

Overview

Dungeness is windswept, bleak and desolate. If it's sunny, there is no shade anywhere, and if it

rains or blows a gale, you'd better be properly dressed. It's a bizarre end-of-the-world kind of place, and this impression is not helped by odd local fixtures such as the Romney, Hythe and Dymchurch miniature railway. Nearby, and dominating the horizon, is the nuclear power station that is visible for miles around.

Derek Jarman's garden is a private garden belonging to a private residence. It is also quite small – although it looks larger in the photos because there are no boundaries and so it appears to stretch out into the surrounding shingle. Derek Jarman bought Prospect Cottage in 1986, looking for some peace and quiet, and created this unique garden, which has widely influenced garden designers in the last decade or so. Since Jarman's death in 1994, the garden has been tended by his partner Keith Collins.

The term 'sculpture garden' is a broad one. I wanted to include Jarman's garden as an example of an alternative sculpture garden – a quiet, intimate setting as opposed to a large commercial venture. However, for this reason I can't in good conscience encourage people to go and see it. Keith and his neighbours are being driven slowly mad by the number of visitors, not to mention that people knock things over, tread on plants and generally disrupt the careful arrangements of things. People live in Dungeness because it is so secluded; it is on the way to nowhere. However, the garden remains a tribute to Derek Jarman

and for that reason Keith has agreed to it being featured. My suggestion would be to enjoy the pictures, be inspired, and perhaps go and set up your own sculpture garden somewhere else.

Derek Jarman was a well-established, highly individual filmmaker before his illness and premature death. His films included Caravaggio (1986), The Garden (1990) and Blue (1993). The cottage was bought from a fisherman who used to sell crabs and shrimps. A keen gardener since childhood, Jarman began the garden in a small way, hoping that at least some plants would survive the strong winds and lack of soil. With time and care, the garden grew and blossomed in surprising and unlikely ways. Against all the odds, a fig tree thrives at the back of the cottage. The sculptures are very much collections of things found on the beach, put to new uses or arranged in patterns. Large stones are laid out into circular flower beds, or form small stone islands in the shingle. Large wooden posts are planted at intervals with rusty metal cappings, breaking up the horizontal beach with slightly phallic-looking vertical shapes. Pebbles punctured by holes are threaded onto metal poles. Old broken and rusting tools have been reinvented as sculptural pieces whose fascinating surfaces can be seen amongst the plants. My favourite things are the small wigwams of twisted metal poles, which apparently were once posts for anti-tank fencing put up during the Second World War. Wild red poppies,

foxgloves and cornflowers are amongst some of the flowers that bloom at various times, throwing a splash of colour against the green sea kale and the endless expanse of shingle. Dungeness is a strange place with an otherworldly charm of its own, and perhaps this is why the garden has such allure as a little haven at the end of the world.

Wooden posts, stones and rusty tools are used to create sculptural arrangements. *Photos by Alison Stace.*

opposite page: *Blue Man* by Clare Ferguson-Walker at 'Art in the Garden'. Resin.

26 'Art in the Garden' at Sir Harold Hillier's Gardens

Information:

Jermyns Lane, Ampfield, Romsey, Hampshire, SO51 0QA.
Tel: 01794 369 317
www.hillier.hants.gov.uk

Facilities: Toilets, two cafés, educational events.
Open: June–end Oct (check for exact dates), 10am–6pm daily.
Admission: Adults £7.50, concessions £6.50, children (under 16) free.
Time needed: 4 hours

Getting there

By road

From the M3, at jct 11 take the A3090 past Hursley and Ampfield towards Romsey, then look for a right turn (follow the brown signposts).
OR
From the M27, take jct 3 onto the A3057 towards Romsey, turn right onto the A3090, then look for a left turn (follow brown signposts).

By train

From Romsey station take a taxi (approx. 10 mins), or bus 32/33, which stops in Braishfield Rd (10 min walk), or bus 35 (Wilts & Dorset Bus Company) which will stop in Braishfield Rd on request.

Overview

'Art in the Garden' at Sir Harold Hillier Gardens, now in its eighth year, is an interesting collaboration between the gardens and Underground Art & Design, who use the fantastic location as a venue for an annual selling exhibition. The enterprise is supported by Hampshire County Council and various commercial sponsors. The extensive gardens (180 acres) were begun in 1953 when Sir Harold and his family moved into Jermyn's House. In 1977 Hillier gave the arboretum to Hampshire County Council to be used as a charitable trust. The sculptures are spread out across the beautifully kept gardens and land, which varies enormously as you go round, and includes fields with wild grass, a formal and carefully planted 'winter garden' with winding paths, a large pond, an avenue of magnolias, and the centenary border – a grass walk with a very tidy array of colourful plants and flowers on either side. Sculptures are also to be found on the vista, a large and open area sloping downhill, offering lovely views. In all this abundance there are some 200 sculptures – and I defy anyone but the organisers to find all of them in one visit. There is a printed list of artists and their work, but the sculptures

are not located on the map, which in any case is a challenge to follow. There is no set route, although occasionally a small sign will point you onwards, and the list does include an area code to help you navigate (for example, OF is Oak Field). But there is no way you will see everything in one visit, so resign yourself to a giant sculpture treasure hunt. Some works are large pieces located in the oak field, which involves a fair amount of walking, while at other times you can find many small works hidden together in flowerbeds. Allow about four hours to see about three quarters of what's there, depending on your speed, and leave extra time for refreshments at the very modern reception building or, better still, have tea on the lawn at the attractive Jermyn's House.

Things to see

The show is curated by Elizabeth Hodgson of Underground Art & Design, a non-profit organisation aimed at promoting artists. Overall, the work here is very modern, using a wide variety of media. Amongst the more unusual were a tree trunk made of tightly-packed paper by Tracey Falcon, and a hilarious pirate scene including captain, hats, cannon and fighting pirates, all made life-size entirely from cardboard, a temporary exhibit made by artist-in-residence David McDiarmid. Obviously, the work changes each year, but pieces that stood out included a spectacular coloured wire dragon by Simply Rewired, and a shining globular form, *Budding*, which resembled a giant seed or pollen grain covered in a mosaic of glass pieces which both glittered and reflected the greenery around it. Julieann Worrall-Hood's *Harum Scarum* series of wire and willow hares leapt and fought superbly above the long grass, while Faith Bebbington's *Falling Men* performed shining silver acrobatics suspended from the trees. For sheer originality the *Sheep Installation* by Katie Lake got my vote – made from wire, concrete and turf, these animals had actual grass growing out of them and little sheep heads. All in all, a comprehensive collection from a wide range of up-and-coming artists.

far left: *Sheep Installation*, by Katie Lake. Concrete and steel. *Photos by Alison Stace.*
middle: *Falling Men*, by Faith Bebbington. Coloured resin.
left: *Budding*, by Rebecca Newnham.

The South-east

27 The Garden Gallery

Information:

Rookery Lane, Broughton, Stockbridge,
Hampshire, SO20 8AZ.
Tel: 01794 301144
www.gardengallery.uk.com

Facilities: None.
Open: Mid-May to end of July (check for
exact dates) or at other times by arrangement.
Admission: Voluntary donation £2 (for local
charity – Wessex Children's Hospice Trust).
Time needed: 30 mins–1 hour

Getting there

By road
• From jct 8 of the M3 take the A303, then
take the A30 to Stockbridge. • Go through
Stockbridge village and follow the A30 towards Salisbury. • Turn left before Lopcombe Corner onto a lane signposted to
Broughton. • At Broughton go through the
village, turning left past the church and
shop, then left onto Rookery Lane. The
gallery is the fifth house along on your left
(called 'Grandfather's House').

By train
The nearest stations are Winchester (best
from London Waterloo), Salisbury (from the
West Country) and Romsey (for the south
coast – Brighton, etc.). Winchester and Salisbury are 20 mins away by taxi and Romsey is 15 mins.

Overview

The Garden Gallery is based in a classic English country garden, complete with small orchard, pond and outhouse, as befits the pretty and traditional village it is located in. The sculpture gallery has been open for 13 years, with work changing all the time. Although some pieces are here all year round, the gallery puts on its main selling exhibition every summer, with the garden divided up into various 'rooms' and work distributed amongst them. These rooms are in fact different pockets and areas of the garden loosely divided by hedges or fences. The garden and most of the sculpture is relatively domestic in scale, with only a few really large pieces, and the work is all of high quality. The larger pieces are mostly located in the paddock, which is also home to the resident friendly horse.

The majority of the work here (and also the strongest) is abstract, making a nice change from many of the smaller venues. Every year, a variety of established artists (approximately

left: *Lily,* by Brian Taylor FRBS. Bronze, life-size. *Photos by Rachel Bebb.*
below: *From Past Memory IV,* by Richard Jackson. Hand-polished cast glass with carved details, stainless steel base.

Things to see

70 are represented, but they do not all show every year), plus five new ones, have work on display here. Pieces are numbered with small ceramic buttons (look closely for these) which correspond to a list of names of works and artists. The garden is not big enough to need a map or get lost in, and sculptures are not positioned numerically. It really is a case of wandering around and seeing what catches your eye. Allow about half an hour to an hour.

far left: *Once Again* by Jonathan Leslie. Verde Indiano marble, Belgian black marble bases.
left: *Nothing Else* by Jacquiline Antonier Creswell (bronze, edition of 7). *Photos by Rachel Bebb.*

You can expect to see the organic bronzes of Charlotte Mayer and the stone carvings of Jonathan Loxley, both regular exhibitors at the gallery. There were two impressive large pieces here by Loxley: *Portal III* is a simple two-metre-tall, gently curved piece of onyx; and *Portal* is a very large freestanding square sculpture fixed into the ground on a corner, to stand in a diamond shape, made (unusually for Loxley) from wire stretched over an aluminium frame, criss-crossing and forming a hole in the centre. Some 14,000 solder joints were required to make this piece.

Wendy Hoare's large pots and Jonathan Barrett-Danes's funky chickens stood out among the ceramic pieces, Richard Jackson's glass piece *From Past Memory IV* was one I enjoyed, similar to the one shown at Newby Hall as well as a more unusual work, *Guarding the Heart*, which combined glass and steel fixings to create intriguing shapes. Other interesting bronzes were *On Tears and Pain 2*, by Helen Sinclair, a very direct and expressive figure of a woman in a skirt, as well as Brian Taylor's dog *Lily* and Deirdre Hubbard's abstract forms.

above left: *Ebb and Flow* by Mat Chivers. Carrara marble, oak plinth. *Photo by Mat Chivers.*
above right: *Split Sphere* by Deirdre Hubbard FRBS. Bronze, oak base, edition of 8. *Photo by Rachel Bebb.*

28 The Gibberd Garden

Information:

Marsh Lane, Gilden Way, Harlow, Essex,
CM17 0NA.
Tel: 01279 442112
www.thegibberdgarden.co.uk

Facilities: Café, toilets, educational
workshops
Opening: Easter–end Sept, 2–6pm Wed,
Sat, Sun & Bank Hols
Admission: Adults £4, concessions £2.50,
children under 16 free.
Time needed: 1½–2 hours

Getting there

By road
• From M11, take jct 7 onto A414 towards
Harlow and Hertford. • Turn right onto
B183 after Church Langley. • Go over two
roundabouts and then look for brown sign
on right (turn into Marsh Lane on left)
before you reach Sheering.

By train
Harlow Mill station then approx. 7 mins by
taxi, or Harlow Town station then 10 mins
by taxi.

Fountain, by Raef Baldwin. Copper pipe and sheet.
Photo courtesy of Gibberd Garden Trust.

Overview

Sir Frederick Gibberd was Harlow's chief town planner and lived for the rest of his life in the town he designed. When he died in 1984, he left the garden to the people of Harlow 'for recreation and education'. Situated on a gently sloping hill, at the bottom of which runs Pincey Brook, with a little 'castle' and moat, the garden's different areas are divided from each other by careful planting and paths. There is also a pond, gazebo and small waterfall. Now run by the Gibberd Trust, which has carried out an extensive programme of restoration, the garden plays host to an eclectic mix of sculpture, most of which was chosen and placed by Frederick Gibberd and his second wife, and is permanently located here. Work is not for sale. The house was originally built in 1907. Gibberd bought it in 1957 and, despite being the town planner, was denied permission to rebuild it. Instead he set about improving and extending it, designing and redesigning – a pattern that continued throughout his landscaping project.

Salvaged columns from Coutts bank on the Strand, London. *Photo by Alison Stace.*

Things to see

Most of the 80 or so sculptures here are classic and traditional, though there are also more modern pieces. Along more traditional lines were the simple stone torso on the lawn by John Skelton, and the very unexpected stone columns and urns from Coutts Bank in the Strand, which he acquired while redesigning it. On a more abstract level, by the pond the welded steel bird, by Hebe Comerford, is very good, as is the copper-pipe fountain by the house, by Raef Baldwin, which looks like the ingenious construction of a mad scientist. On a more contemporary note, the large shining silver *Owl* by Antanas Brazdys stands out against a dark hedge, and Monica Young's coiled pot is set off by a 'Zen garden' of carefully laid pebbles. Other artists with work here include David Nash, Gerda Rubenstein and Zadok Ben David. The garden is 16 acres, although some of this is given over to the brook, so allow about an hour and a half to look around.

far left: *Lucinda*, by Gerda Rubenstein.
middle: *Bird*, by Hebe Comerford. Welded mild steel.
left: *Owl*, by Antanas Brazdys. Stainless steel.

29 Bergh Apton Sculpture Trail

Information:

Village of Bergh Apton
Tel: 01508 550119
www.berghapton.org.uk

Facilities: Toilets and refreshments available
Open: Several weekends in May & June,
once every three years. The next show is in
2008 on the following dates: 24 & 25 May,
31 May & 1 June, 7 & 8 June, from
10.30am–6pm.
Admission: Adults £10 (2 day ticket £15),
children free.

Getting there

By road
Bergh Apton is just off the A146 which
runs between Norwich and Beccles.

By train
An hour by bus or 20 minutes by taxi from
Norwich station.

right: *The Painter* by Neal French, 2005. Bronze resin.
opposite top left: *Natural Circumference 3,
Standing,* by Dominique Bivar Segurado, 2005.
Stoneware clay mounted on a slate base. *Photo
courtesy of artist.*
bottom left: *Wild Boar* by Harriet Mead, 2005.
Found metals, barbed wire. *Photo by Derek Blake.*
far right: *Angel Wing* by Mel Fraser, 2005. *Photos
courtesy of Bergh Apton Community Arts Trust.*

Overview

This sculpture trail is unusual in being put together only every three years by the village of Bergh Apton – a community effort to bring art and sculpture out of the city galleries and into a rural community – and comprises work by invited artists displayed throughout gardens in the village. The first event was organised in 1997, with the last show (2005) featuring 75 artists showing about 3 pieces each. The next show, in 2008, involves 12 gardens in a four-mile radius around the village, with access only on foot or by bicycle. The trail route changes every show depending on how many gardens are included. The exhibition is organised by the Bergh Apton Community Arts Trust, and any leftover money is ploughed back into the village (for the school, village hall, church and conservation trust). Selected sculptors are invited to exhibit by agreement of the committee, and then visit the village to get ideas for the work they intend to make. The 2008 show, entitled 'Balance', is on the theme of conservation of the environment.

The West Country

• Cornwall • Devon • Somerset • Dorset • Wiltshire

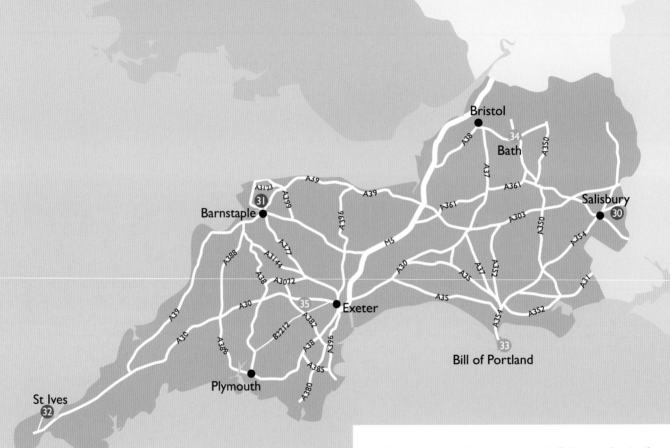

30 New Art Centre Sculpture Park & Gallery at Roche Court
31 Broomhill Art Hotel & Sculpture Gardens
32 Barbara Hepworth Museum & Sculpture Garden

Other Places of Interest

33 Tout Sculpture Park, Portland Sculpture & Quarry Trust
34 Bristol to Bath Railway Path
35 Mythic Garden

30 New Art Centre Sculpture Park & Gallery

Information:

Roche Court, East Winterslow, Salisbury,
Wiltshire, SP5 1BG.
Tel: 01980 862244
www.sculpture.uk.com

Facilities: There are toilets, but no café here.
As always, local pubs provide food and facilities.
Educational programmes.
Open: 11am–4pm
Admission: Free
Time needed: 1½–2 hours

Getting there

By road or helicopter

As cannot be said for most parks, this one offers a helicopter landing area for the wealthier collector's convenience! • If your helicopter is currently out of action however, and driving or cycling seems more likely, coming **by road from Salisbury** on the A30, you will pass the Pheasant pub on your left. • The road you need is signposted about a mile further along on your right. Follow the signs for Roche Court.
• **Coming from Stockbridge** along the same road, shortly after Lopcombe Corner, where the A30 meets the A343, turn left onto the small road signposted to Roche Court. • A lane leads you to an unobtrusive car park, and suddenly it is not at all clear that you are in the right place. The park begins at the house, which you can see from the car park lower down through the trees. At the side of the house is a gateway into the grounds.

By train

From Salisbury station, it's about 20 minutes by taxi.

Overview

This prestigious sculpture park has a long list of artists associated with it, including many famous names that have exhibited here over the years. It always has an impressive array of work, and though the grounds are much smaller than, say, YSP or Goodwood, they are beautiful. However, as with both of these parks, the standard of work is exceptional. All works shown are for sale, and thus the inventory of pieces is liable to change. Artists to have displayed work here include William Turnbull, Antony Gormley, Richard Long, Richard Deacon and Antony Caro. The centre is also the sole representative of Barbara Hepworth, managing both her estate and any exhibitions of her work around the world, and there are always a few of her pieces on display.

The New Art Centre was founded by Madeleine Bessborough in 1958, originally as a gallery in Sloane Street in London. In 1994, it relocated to Roche Court, a 19th-century house (not open to visitors) and gardens in a beautiful and secluded setting perfect for wandering around. The views are also worth taking in. The staff at the centre are very enthusiastic, helpful and knowledgeable about all the artists on display. When we arrived on a very wet afternoon, we were greeted at the door of the house with enormous umbrellas that they keep handy for visitors on these occasions. The award-winning gallery, designed by architects Munkenbeck and Marshall, part of which was originally the orangery, has one side made entirely from glass. Exhibitions in the gallery change about four times a year.

The centre has recently added to the estate by building a small house behind the original building. This impressive piece of modern architecture, also designed by Stephen Marshall, is built from frameless glass, oak and stone, and was designed as an artist's residence for visiting artists working on projects in the park. It holds further artworks, including pieces by Lucian Freud, Nina Saunders and Barbara Hepworth, and three fantastic large ceramic jars in the hidden courtyard by Rupert Spira. It is always nice to see large-scale ceramics in a sculptural context, and these are perfectly suited to the calm, monastic atmosphere of this setting. However, it is important to note that the artists' house can only be viewed by appointment arranged in advance.

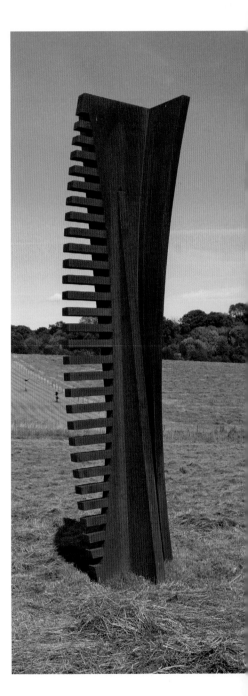

previous page: *Acrobats*, by Barry Flanagan, 2000. Bronze.
right: *Stretched Diagonals* by Nigel Hall, 2003. Cor-Ten™ Steel.
Photos courtesy of New Art Centre.

Finding your way around

Maps of the garden are provided with numbers locating the position of sculptures, along with a sheet listing all the corresponding numbered pieces. If nobody is in the house or office, maps are available from the shelf on the porch of the house. The map system works well as the park is a manageable size. There were approximately 50 sculptures on display in the grounds, and it took us about an hour and a half to see everything. The furthest flung piece is Barry Flanagan's *Acrobats*, located over the stile and across a field, and well worth the walk. Be careful not to miss the rest of the sculptures on your return, as some of them are located just inside the small wooded area and are harder to spot.

left: *Tame Buzzard Line* by Richard Long, 2001. Flint. *Photo courtesy of New Art Centre.*

Things to see

Sculptures at the New Art Centre are always likely to change, but there are always pieces worth seeing. A few worth mentioning are Barry Flanagan's fantastic *Acrobats*, Richard Long's impressive land art in the form of *Tame Buzzard Line*, a line of stones leading your eye towards a large tree at the bottom of the field. David Nash has recently had work here: in 2006 he showed *Three Humps*, and in 2007 *Two Eggs*. Both Nash and Long work in natural materials and their work blends in well with the surrounding landscape. Some of Anthony Caro's work is still on display after his exhibition here in 2007. Kenneth Armitage has also had work here of abstract bronzes, as well as Laura Ford, whose surreal bronze *Bird*, a giant bird (possibly a crow) with a child's legs, is both unnerving and fascinating at the same time. It looks like a hybrid of bird/human that is struggling to resolve who or what it should be, and is instead trapped in between two forms. An early piece of her work on the hybrid theme can be seen at Chiltern sculpture Trail (see p.114). As previously mentioned, there are

above: *Two Figures,* by Barbara Hepworth, 1968. Bronze with colour.
right above: *Toronto Flat* by Anthony Caro, 1974 (from '12 Flats' series). Steel.
right below: *Wrapt* by Ellis O'Connell, 1999. Bronze, edition 3 of 3.
Photos courtesy of New Art Centre.

usually a few pieces of Hepworth's work on display. There are also impressive pieces inside the gallery, which has recently featured Richard Deacon. New work is always arriving from the many well-known artists that show here, and if you are interested in specific artists you can check on their well organised website for information on past pieces as well as current work before visiting.

31 Broomhill Art Hotel & Sculpture Gardens

Information:

Muddiford, Barnstaple, North Devon,
EX31 4EX.
Tel: (00 44) 01271 850262
www.broomhillart.co.uk

Facilities: Toilets, restaurant, gallery, hotel.
Opening: All year (CHK), Wed, Thu, Fri, Sat &
Sun, 11am – 4pm
(4pm is the last admission time)
Admission: Adults £4.50, children £1.50,
concessions £3.50, family group (2 adults,
2 children) £10.
Time needed: 1½ hours

Getting there

By road

Take M5 to jct 27, then take the A361 to
Barnstaple. • From Barnstaple take the
A39 towards Lynton. Turn left soon after-
wards onto the B3230. The Broomhill Art
Hotel is on your left (signposted) before
you reach Muddiford.

By train

Barnstaple station then approx. 15 minutes
by taxi.

By coach

Coaches run from London (Victoria) and the
Midlands to Barnstaple.

Overview

Reminiscent of the Hannah Peschar Sculpture Garden, with its many twisty paths, ponds and hidden areas, Broomhill is both a wonderfully stylish modern hotel set in an old building and a comprehensive sculpture garden. It was a major undertaking to turn the previously neglected building into a hotel with restaurant and gallery, and the wild grounds into a garden with staggered terraces, paths and stairs. Built up over the last 11 years by its enthusiastic and charismatic owners, Rinus van de Sande has put together an amazing array of work by a wide variety of sculptors – many of whom are unknown. Despite this, the standard of work is very high, and as Rinus points out, 'The English are all obsessed with artists

being known or unknown, but there is often very little difference between a known artist and an unknown artist. A known artist is simply someone who has been lucky enough to be taken up and promoted by a wealthy client or gallery.'

As with the majority of sculpture parks, all the art here is for sale, and therefore subject to change. It is quite bronze-dominated, with a strong element of figurative work. The hotel is situated at the top of the hill, and the winding paths divide the hill into several levels as they descend. At the bottom of the hill a river flows through the garden, lending the setting a peaceful soundtrack. The garden is well managed,

with most pieces carefully placed in prominent positions to make the most of their location, while others remain semi-hidden, surprising you as you round a corner.

As the Broomhill Art Hotel also serves lunch and tea, you can combine your visit with some refreshments. The very interesting mix of sculpture in this beautiful setting makes it well worth a visit.

opposite: *Keeping,* by Antonia Spowers. Mild steel, copper and wire.
below left: *Pond Life,* by David Kemp. Recycled water bottles, mild-steel rods and solar lights.
below right: *Red Stiletto,* by Greta Berlin. Resin coat.

Finding your way around

The many trees, but especially the steep hill, make this garden harder to navigate than some, so that descending lower than the top level is not for those with buggies or for anyone unsteady on their feet. As there is no set route around the park, it is easy to miss interesting parts of the garden, making it necessary to criss-cross your path and backtrack occasionally in order to see everything. All the sculptures are labelled with small signs to tell you the name of the work and artist. It takes about an hour to see everything.

Things to see

The top level of the garden cleverly offers an even grassy terrace on which many small sculptures are displayed, a great idea as smaller sculptures can often get lost in large parks. There is a strong element of figurative work, with amongst the many interesting smaller pieces *Equilibrium*, by Dorothy Brook, being well displayed against the backdrop of treetops, doing gymnastics in the air and balancing carefully on one hand from her plinth. The striking blue of this sculpture stood out well against the treetops and sky.

The Three Graces, by Joanna Mallin-Davies, cavort effortlessly in the nude, and looked both rapturous and peaceful. They seem to create their own private world, and reminded me of a witch's coven. Anna Gillespie's small boy (ironically entitled *Strong Man*) looks lost in his own thoughts as he contemplates the ground. A quietly powerful emotional presence, it is also unusually constructed, initially from masking tape which creates the interesting surface, before a mould is taken in rubber and it is cast in bronze.

A recent acquisition, the three tall yellow Oriental figures entitled *Artists of The Silk Road* by Laury Dizengremel, stand at the bottom of the hill near the large pond, dominating the space and competing with the trees in height. The fascinating and beautiful faces were perfectly formed and frighteningly realistic, while the shapes of their bodies could just be faintly made out through the roughly formed torsos, which resembled swathes of cloaks, kimonos or wrappings.

The entire area occupied by the old tennis courts had (at the time) been turned over to Mike Roles for an exhibition developed over several years and entitled *Welcome to the Third Millennium*, a scene invoking concentration camps and chemical warfare with figures in gas masks and bandaged hands kneeling on the ground or slumped in chairs, half-disintegrated. Not surprisingly, the artist turns out also to be a philosopher, and his work deals with life, death, time and decay. The long-term plan for this area is to hold a series of changing exhibitions here.

far left: *Artists of The Silk Road* by Laury Dizengremel.
middle: *Strong Man* by Anna Gillespie, 2005. Bronze.
left: *Welcome to the Third Millenium* (detail), by Mike Roles. *Photos by Alison Stace.*
right: *Manbetu* by Diane Gorvin. Cold-cast painted resin, life-size. *Photo courtesy of Broomhill Sculpture Garden.*

32 Barbara Hepworth Museum & Sculpture Garden

Information:

Barnoon Hill, St Ives, Cornwall, TR26 1TG.
Tel: 01736 796226
tate.org.uk/stives/hepworth

Facilities: Toilets
Open: Mar–Oct, 10am–5.20pm every day,
Nov–Feb, 10am–4.20pm (closed Mon).
Admission: adults £4.75, concessions £2.75,
free for under 18s and over 60s.

Getting there

By road

• At end M5 (jct 31) pick up the A30 and
continue west through Devon and Cornwall. • After signs for Redruth & Cam-
borne turn right onto the A3074 into St
Ives. • There are several car parks in St
Ives, so if traffic is heavy, park at the first
one with spaces and walk into the centre
on foot (or park near the Tate). Small signs
point you to the museum from the end of
the main shopping street.

By train

St Ives station (from Paddington, London)
and a 10 to 15-minute walk.

right: *Four Square (Walk Through)*, 1966.
far right: *River Form*, 1965. *Photos by Alison
Stace, by permission of the Hepworth Estate.*

Overview

St Ives is a small but picturesque coastal town complete with bars, shops and cobbled streets, much like a miniature version of Brighton. Despite its size, it is easy to get lost among the maze of little roads, and since every other person is a tourist, it's hard to get directions too. The museum and garden are located a very short distance (a 10-minute walk) from Tate St Ives. The entrance looks like an old-fashioned door to a tiny town house, which is exactly what this building is. Step through the narrow doorway and you enter the house that Hepworth lived in. The garden is a considerable size in comparison to the house, and very well hidden. You would have no idea of its size from the outside, and indeed Hepworth herself wrote that she had been passing the walls for ten years with no idea that her perfect studio and garden lay on the other side. She acquired it in 1949 and lived there until her tragic death in a fire in 1975. The studios, which are built into the hill, one leading to the next, occupy at least as much space as the house, so it is easy to see what took priority in her life. 'Trewyn studio and garden' were once part of Trewyn House next door. The garden is well established now, and paths lead you around the small pond and impressive trees. The garden seems a strange hybrid, with parts giving off the air of a Mediterranean garden with a seated area against a painted wall and tall exotic trees, while the rest is an English country garden, with roses and a stone bridge leading over the pond. Although a private space, Hepworth also used the garden to display her works, both for her own creative purposes and for visiting gallery owners and buyers.

Finding your way around

The museum and garden is pretty small, so no map is needed, and the sculptures are all identified with numbered plaques. A leaflet lists all the works with corresponding numbers. Firm, constructed paths lead you easily around the well-maintained garden, which although on a hill is relatively flat, aside from a few steps here and there. Pieces have been situated with great care to relate to other forms and textures within the garden. Well-placed benches allow you to sit and enjoy the tranquillity of the space.

Things to see

It is easy to see everything here, and indeed you should, in order to get a well-rounded view of Hepworth's work as it changed over time. The elegant, curved and natural shapes reflect her love of the landscape, while her use of strings described the interior of forms in a different way. Listed below are a few of the pieces in the garden that I particularly liked, although every piece is worth reflecting upon. Her work is occasionally out on loan for exhibitions, so some pieces may be missing.

Four Square (Walk Through) is one of the largest pieces, and also one of the first things you see on the lawn as you come out of the house. Hepworth made it in 1966, almost as a reaction to being diagnosed with cancer the year before. The viewer was originally invited to engage with the sculpture by passing through its centre. The squareness of this vast piece is broken up by the circles that allow glimpses of sky and garden as the viewer walks through and round, offering all sorts of combinations of shapes and framed views, enabling the work to achieve a kind of equilibrium. Its strong architecture is also softened by the interaction of the viewer with the garden.

Two Forms (Divided Circle), is another large and perfectly balanced form – perfectly balanced with itself and the landscape, because the holes and the two halves themselves are not identical at all: one has another oval cut around the circle within, giving more depth to the form. Originally, the inside faces of the holes would have been a polished gold colour, drawing more focus to the edges and the spaces themselves. What makes the circle join is the viewer's perception.

River Form, also situated on the grass area, collects water within its hollow interior, while the holes in the sides suggest water flowing in and out. The painted inside also hints at

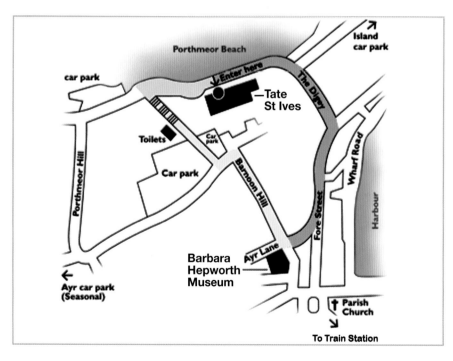

opposite: *Conversation with Magic Stones,* 1973. Bronze. *Photo by Marcus Leith,* © *Bowness, Hepworth Estate.*
left: Map by Tate Museum and Joe Knight.

water and lightens the interior. One of my favourite pieces, it has an essentially soothing quality about it. This work was actually cast from a carved wooden mould.

Sea Form (Porthmeor), located inside one of the studios, is actually the plaster mould that was used to cast an edition of seven bronzes. It has been painted a deceptive bronzed colour – perhaps to give an indication to a buyer of how the finished work would look. This natural form evokes the sea – Porthmeor is the name of a local beach – and the shape is reminiscent of both a breaking wave and a seashell.

Conversations with Magic Stones is a very large piece consisting of three large upright works and three smaller ones, all standing in relation to each other. The three larger upright pieces seem to represent figures, an impression based both on their appearance and on things Hepworth wrote about her work. The relationship between them reflects human interaction, while the smaller stones (the 'Magic' stones) obviously represent mystical forces. Hepworth was fascinated by standing stones found in the landscape, and obviously felt drawn to them, as this work seems to express.

above: *Two Forms (Divided Circle)*, 1969. Bronze. *Photo by Bob Berry, © Bowness, Hepworth Estate.* **below:** *Sea Form (Porthmeor)*, 1958. Bronze. *Photo by unknown photographer, © Bowness, Hepworth Estate.*

The West Country

Other Places of Interest

33 Tout Sculpture Park – Portland Sculpture & Quarry Trust

A Tear for Stone, by anonymous carver. *Photo by Alison Stace, with permission of PSQT.*

Information:

Office address: The Drill Hall, Portland, Dorset, DT5 1BW.
Tel: 01305 826736
www.learningstone.org

Facilities: None on site, but check out the wonderful Sugar Loaf Café in the nearby village of Easton (with an extensive range of great food).
Summer workshops.
Open: All year
Admission: Free
Time needed: 2–2½ hours

Getting there

Tout Sculpture Park is located in a disused quarry on the strange Isle of Portland, a spit of land off the coast of Dorset. This odd sculpture park is actually quite hard to find, and it doesn't help that, despite all the official information calling it the Portland Sculpture Trust, all the signs point you to the Tout Sculpture Park. The Isle itself has a very eerie feel, with all roads seeming to lead back to either the main road or the Bill of Portland, a viewing point at the far end of the island. The quarry is signposted from one direction only. The whole system seems to have been set up to allow visitors in but not out again.

By road

Take the A354 via Weymouth to the Isle of Portland across the narrow spit of land joining it to the mainland. • Once in Portland, drive through the residential area of Fortuneswell. The road takes you up a steep hill with hairpin bends, past sculptures of a fisherman and quarry worker, and one of the huge structures used for lifting stone. • At the roundabout at the top of the hill, take the third exit along Wide Street, then turn right into what looks like an industrial park (known as Tradecroft) with a Royal Mail office on the corner. • At the end of this road, bear right onto a pitted gravel road. It looks derelict, but eventually you will come to some laminated boards on the left, bearing a map of the park, you can park opposite.

By train

Weymouth station and then 15 mins by taxi or a bus ride (bus X10, approx. 30 mins, frequent buses in summer, reduced service in winter).

Overview

At the first laminated board along the gravel road a tiny unmarked path leads off to your left between the bushes, and takes you down towards the quarry. The whole place looks as if it hasn't been visited for 1000 years; in reality, the quarry has been disused for about 75 years, but it was not until 1983 that artists were invited to create works here in order to keep the site active. Portland stone is world-famous, used in architecture and sculpture in cities everywhere, and the skills and knowledge needed to work the stone by hand were passed down through many generations of local men. Now sculpture workshops are held here in the summer, and the students make use of the leftover stone to create new pieces, so the amount of sculpture is always increasing (see website for details on booking workshops).

It has to be said that the sculpture here is not always the most exciting you will ever see, although there are some good pieces. It is a great example, however, of a truly integrated land-and-art concept, where the artists come to make the work *in situ* from the material found on site (as opposed to making work in a studio from other materials and then transporting it for display). It gives a direct meaning to the notion of art in landscape. The place is also worth a visit just for the experience of visiting the atmospheric disused quarry. There are now 53 sculptures here, and at the time of our visit the laminated maps were in the process of being redesigned to show them all marked on the route. However, as they are made from the same stone that surrounds them, you need to vigilant. Suddenly you will realise that a strange-looking boulder is actually the figure of a crouching man, or that drawings have been etched into a rock you are leaning against. It is part of the enjoyment of the place that many of the sculptures are almost hidden, waiting to be discovered.

opposite page: *Still Falling*, by Antony Gormley, 1983. Incised into rockface *in situ*.
far left: *Be Stone No More* by Pierre Vivant.
left: *Fallen Fossil* by Stephen Marsden, 1985.
Photos courtesy of Portland Sculpture Quarry Trust.

Finding your way around

The Tout Sculpture Park is essentially un-manned, so there are no paper maps provided, but regular information points using laminated boards show you where you are and where the sculptures are located. These were recently due to be updated to show the 53 sculptures hidden amongst the stone. Most are found away from the main path, but these detours are well worth the trouble, as there are also many un-official carvings on stones in unexpected places. Although the quarry seems vast, you can't go very far wrong with the sea on one side and the road on the other. The workshop area is also a good landmark.

Things to see

Amongst the official sculptures, Shelagh Wakely's *Representation of a Baroque Garden* was one of the best and was also first on the route. Obscured by giant boulders on the quarry floor, it is best viewed from above by climbing the small raised path around it heading towards the sea. Tucked away inside the quarry and also quite hard to spot is Antony Gormley's *Still Falling*, which almost catches you unawares but is perfectly situated, carved onto a bare patch of rock on the far side of a chasm. Half-floating and half-falling, the surreal figure heads down into a dip towards what looks almost like a natural hidden doorway in the rock. How Gormley managed to reach that spot to carve anything at all is a feat in itself. Nearby, *Hearth* is a beautifully carved, very realistic fireplace looking like it just needs some coal to get it started. I also liked *Crouching Figure*, which could so easily be a strange-shaped boulder until it suddenly clicks into place and the recognisable shape of a person emerges from the rock. The *Arena of Fools* was also quite intriguing, with its cave-like drawings on various boulders surrounding an open area. *Fallen Fossil*, *Be Stone No More* and *Ascent* are other interesting pieces which work particularly well with their surroundings. Finally, be sure to walk through the stone archway and look out for *A Tear for Stone*, a man's face carved into the face of the stone along the path on your right.

left: *Lizard,* by John Roberts. *Photo courtesy of Portland Sculpture & Quarry Trust.*
right: *Mangotsfield Window Grills,* by Katy Hallett, installed at Mangotsfield station on the Brisol to Bath Railway Path. *Photo by Alison Stace.*

The West Country

34 Bristol to Bath Railway Path

Information:

Tel: 0845 113 0065
www.bristolbathrailwaypath.org.uk

Facilities: Public toilets available at Bath and Bristol stations, and at Bitton station on the route. Bitton station also has a café.
Open: All year
Admission: Free
Time needed: 3 hours (by bicycle)

1a **Sleeper Seat** by Jim Partridge and Liz Walmsley
2 **Drinking Stone** by Michael Fairfax
3 **Wind-blown Oak Seat** by Jim Partridge and Liz Walmsley
4 **Owl Pole** by Dominic Lowrey
5 **Stone Carvings Saxon Relics** by Nick Moore
6 **On the Wing** by Vizability Arts
7 **Gaius Sentinus drinking fountain** by Gordon Young
8 **Brief Encounters** by Steve Joyce
9 **Carved Timber Bench** by Will Glanfield
10 **Mangotsfield Window Grills** by Katy Hallett
11 **Green Canopy** by John Grimshaw
12 **Sentinel I & II** byProfessor Jim
a&b Paulsen
13 **Mosaic Mural** by Vizability Arts
14 **Fish on its Nose** by Doug Cocker
1b **Sleeper Seat** by Jim Partridge and Liz Walmsley
15 **British Gas Milepost** (1 of 5) – to celebrate British Gas Working for Cities Public Art Award
16 **Easton Railings** by Barbara Disney and Kevin Hughes
17 **Dancing Drum** by Steve Joyce
18 **Twisted Arch Gateway** by Cod Steaks

Map courtesy of Sustrans and Joe Knight

The West Country

Getting There

By road
• **To start from Bristol**, take the M4 and come off at jct 19 onto M32. Follow signs to Temple Meads station from the centre. You can park at the station, although it does get busy.
• **To start from Bath**, take the M4 to jct 18 and come off onto the A46, then follow signs to Bath centre, and the train station (near the river and A367). You can park at the station.

By train
From Bristol Temple Meads or Bath Spa stations, then see directions below to start of path.

By steam train
This goes through Bitton, Oldlands and Avon Riverside. www.avonvalleyrailway.org/index.shtml

On bicycle (or foot) from Bristol
The route begins at the end of St Philips Road in Bristol, and is a 5-minute cycle from Temple Meads railway station across the new curving pedestrian bridge. (New signposts are going up to help people find the path from the station.) • From Temple Meads train station, come out onto Avon Street (back entrance) turn right, and then left onto Midland Rd, then left onto St Philips Rd. The path starts at the end of St Philips Rd. A new sculptural gateway has been installed recently.

On bicycle (or foot) from Bath
Come out of Bath train station and turn left, cycle straight along this road until you come to a large junction where it crosses the river. • Do not cross the river, but continue straight on, along the right-hand side of the canal. You will see a small path leading off to your left which runs along the towpath. • Follow this until you come to the Dolphin pub (the only pub on this stretch) and then come back up onto the road at the bridge, staying to the right of the canal again. You will see signs directing you from here to the railway path. You can take the train back from either end.

Overview

This is actually a cycle route (Cycle Network number 4), and the sculptures have been commissioned by Sustrans which manages large numbers of cycle paths across England. Many routes have sculptures (some commissioned, some just incorporated into the route), including some by Andy Goldsworthy (Three Rivers Cycle route). There are approx. 300 sculptures along the combined routes. This is the first route that was developed. You can also walk the railway path, but be warned that they do get a lot of use by cyclists, especially at weekends. The Bath to Bristol trail is actually 13 miles long, but allowing for getting to and from stations at both ends it is more like 16 miles. Most of the sculpture along the route is between Bristol and Bitton, so if you are short of time and energy you could just do that section (about 9 miles). Bitton station is also a good place to stop as it has toilets, and a café serving hot food and sandwiches, with outdoor seating. There is also a steam train that runs through Bitton station if you prefer to take that (check website, see left). The sculptures do vary a lot in quality, but there were about 15 sculptures along the route, and as it goes along a disused railway line you have the slightly eerie feel of disused stations whose platforms offer ideal space for artworks. I had three favourites: *Brief Encounter* by Steve Joyce, metallic silhouettes of people waiting for trains (at Warmley

Station); near Warmley was *Gaius Sentius* a giant water fountain – literally depicting a giant drinking, made from stone by Gordon Young; and at Mangotsfield station *Window Grills* by Katy Hallett, who has made repeat pattern designs from cut-out pieces of metal across the old windows of the station. Inside the old station (opened in 1869), now just a few walls with arched windows, was a sort of hidden garden, ideal for a picnic stop. Further along the platform was a bronze suitcase and enormous samples of old tickets set into the concrete. The railway path is a lovely walk or cycle way, with loads of greenery and a very friendly atmosphere. The Sustrans off-road routes are a fantastic resource for a bit of R&R with sculptures – you can check their websites for artwork before you set off. This route took about 3 hours by bicycle.

below: *Gaius Sentius Fountain*, by Gordon Young, 1992.
left: *Brief Encounter* (detail), by Steve Joyce. Located at the former Warmley station platform. *Photos courtesy of J. Bewley/Sustrans.*

35 The Mythic Garden

Information:

Stone Lane Gardens, Stone Farm, Chagford, Devon, TQ13 8JU.
Tel: 01647 231311
www.stonelanegardens.com

Facilities: None
Open: Daily from 2–6pm, June–Sept (check for exact start and end dates).
Admission: Adults £4, students & children (aged 5–16) £2.50, children (under 5) free.
Time needed: 1½ hours

Getting there

By road

Come off the A30 at Whiddon Down onto the A382 towards Moretonhampstead, then turn left at the roundabout (following A382). • Take the third left after Chapel Hill and Turnpike Lane, down a narrow lane sign-posted Drewsteignton. • Pass a right turn for Spinster's Rock and take the next right turn. The car park is through the working yard on your left. Then follow signs on foot.

By train and bus

From Exeter St Davids station, take bus 173 from Exeter bus station to Chagford (1 hr) then 172 from Chagford to Whiddon Down, and walk (1.5 miles).

right: *Forest Guardians* by Peter Clarke, 2007. Chestnut/oak/glass. *Photos by Alison Stace.*
middle: *Erect Neck and Bent Neck Swan* by Tony Smither, 2007. Ceramic.
far right: *Unicorn* by Ed Netley, 2007. Wire.

Overview

Every year for four months Stone Lane Gardens becomes the Mythic Garden sculpture exhibition, run privately by the Ashburners. The Stone Lane Gardens were started in 1971 by Kenneth Ashburner, and have gradually been cultivated as part of a scientific project. Set within five acres of a larger woodland of birch and alder trees (officially designated as national collections), the landscaped gardens and woodland have several ponds, three of which feed water by a stream from one to the next. Garden paths of woodchip twist and turn, winding off amongst bushes and trees into hidden corners or over tiny bridges. It is a beautiful place which takes about an hour and a half to wander round.

Things to see

The exhibition, curated by June Ashburner, has been running since 1992. Every year it features new work by a small constant core of West Country artists plus a changing roster of other contributors. With approximately 120 pieces, the exhibition is pretty varied, with plenty of interesting pieces and a strong quota of ceramic work. As the title of the garden exhibition might suggest, the work leans towards being, as June puts it, 'sympathetic to what the garden is trying to achieve'. This means that much of the work has a 'natural' or even 'mystical' theme. Mythic pieces from the 2007 exhibition in-cluded *Pegasus*, by Alicia Castrillo, an im-pressive life-size small winged horse made of steel and willow, and my personal favourite, *Unicorn*, made from wire by Ed Netley. Amongst the many other animal, plant and figurative works there were also some good ceramic *Masks* tied to trees, by Pauline Lee; *Three Flying Swifts*, by Celia Smith (a leading wire artist), which I almost missed as they blended in so well, suspended from a branch; *Poseidon and Demeter*, by Jennie Scott, some great horses' heads in the lower pond; and a giant copper-and-steel spider by Gary and Thomas Thrussel, which stalked menac-ingly amongst the trees in a Harry Pot-teresque fashion. There was also *Vision in the Sky*, by Jane Mowat, a wonderful relief carving of a shadowy figure, made from a slice of oak; and on a more abstract note, the *Forest Guardians* kept watch on every-one with their twenty or so eyes, all growing out of wooden poles amongst the trees.

above left: *Large Mask* by Pauline Lee. Ceramic.
above right: *Free-standing Spider* by Gary & Thomas Thrussel. Copper/bare steel.
Photos by Alison Stace.

Further Places of Interest

Ireland
SCULPTURE IN WOODLAND
Devil's Glen Wood, Ashford, Co. Wicklow, Ireland

Tel: 00 (353) 1 201 1132

www.sculptureinwoodland.ie

Currently 18 artists have been commissioned to make work for Devil's Glen, much of which is on a large to monumental scale, and in natural materials. The work is mainly by Irish artists, as well as some international ones. The first sculptures were installed in 1996. The park covers 600 acres, which was formed by a glacier and much of which is lovely woodland, and includes a waterfall. There are two different sculpture trails, both of which are about 2 miles long and start from the car park. Maps and descriptions of the walks can be found and downloaded from their comprehensive website, as well as a map of how to get there.

Scotland
GLENKILN SCULPTURE
Glenkiln reservoir, Glenkiln, near Dumfries, Dumfries and Galloway

www.walkingworld.com/results/walksummary.
    asp?method=thirdpartyid&twlkno=1764

http://myweb.tiscali.co.uk/celynog/Dumfries/
    sculpture_walk.htm

From the A75, just west of Dumfries, turn off towards Shawhead. At Shawhead turn right then left, and then take the next left towards Glenkiln (signposted). Drive to the reservoir, and park at the end near the Rodin sculpture. The sculptures are located to the left of the road opposite the reservoir. You can print off details of the walk and works, and a map, from the two websites above. The sculptures were bought by Sir William Keswick who owned the land, and placed around the reservoir from 1951–76. The walk has some very good pieces of work by very well-known artists, amongst them Henry Moore, Rodin, and Jacob Epstein. There are also amazing views. The walk is approximately 5 miles and takes 2 hours.

Wales
LAKE VYRNWY SCULPTURE TRAIL
Lake Vyrnwy, Lanwddyn, Powys, Wales

Tel: 01691 870278

www.visitmidwales.co.uk/thedms.asp?dms=13&
    feature=5&venue=1023341

www.stawater.co.uk

From Llanfyllin, take the B4393 to Llanwddyn. Continue along the B4393 to Llanwddyn by turning right. At the dam, turn left, then left at the end of the dam, then look for the RSPB visitor centre on the right. You can park here. The Lake Vyrnwy Symposium has been running since 1999. Every year, sculptors come from across the world to exchange ideas, visit the country and make work from the soft pine supplied by the estate. These sculptures have been installed on the 'island' below the dam, and have gradually accumulated to produce a sculpture park of about 60 works, from both Welsh and international artists. This large collection of international sculpture in the landscape has now filled the space, so the symposium is being relocated but the sculpture park remains open to visitors all year.

Index